# About Reading Connection:

**W**elcome to RBP Books' Connection series. Reading Connection provides students with focused practice to help reinforce and develop reading skills in areas appropriate for fourth-grade students. Reading Connection uses a variety of writing types and exercises to help build comprehension, thinking, phonics, vocabulary, language, reasoning, and other skills important to both reading and critical thinking. In accordance with NCTE (National Council of Teachers of English) standards, reading material and exercises are grade-level appropriate, and clear examples and instructions guide the lesson. Activities help students develop reading skills and give special attention to vocabulary development.

Dear Parents and Educators,

Thank you for choosing this Rainbow Bridge Publishing educational product to help teach your children and students. We take great pride and pleasure in becoming involved with your educational experience. Some people say that math will always be math and reading will always be reading, but we do not share that opinion. Reading, math, spelling, writing, geography, science, history, and all other subjects will always be some of life's most fulfilling adventures and should be taught with passion both at home and in the classroom. Because of this, we at Rainbow Bridge Publishing associate the greatness of learning with every product we create.

It is our mission to provide materials that not only explain, but also amaze; not only review, but also encourage; not only guide, but also lead. Every product contains clear, concise instructions, appropriate sample work, and engaging, grade-appropriate content created by classroom teachers and writers that is based on national standards to support your best educational efforts. We hope you enjoy our company's products as you embark on your adventure. Thank you for bringing us along.

Sincerely,

George Starks
Associate Publisher
Rainbow Bridge Publishing

---

# Reading Connection™ • Grade 4
## Written by Molly McMahon

Illustrations
Jonathan Hallett

Visual Design and Layout
Andy Carlson, Robyn Funk, Zachary Johnson, Scott Whimpey

Publisher
Scott G. Van Leeuwen

Editorial Director
Paul Rawlins

Associate Publisher
George Starks

Copy Editors and Proofreaders
Jennifer Browning, Elaine Clark

Series Creator
Michele Van Leeuwen

Technology Integration
James Morris, Dante J. Orazzi

Please visit our website at
**www.summerbridgeactivities.com**
for supplements, additions, and corrections to this book.

First Edition 2003

For orders call 1-800-598-1441
Discounts available for quantity orders

ISBN: 1-932210-19-9

PRINTED IN THE UNITED STATES OF AMERICA
10 9 8 7 6 5 4 3 2 1

# Table of Contents

# 4th Grade Reading List

**Avi**
Poppy
Poppy and Rye

**Ballard, Robert D.**
Finding the Titanic

**Banks, Lynne Reid**
The Indian in the Cupboard

**Blume, Judy**
Fudge-a-Mania
Tales of a Fourth Grade
Nothing

**Cleary, Beverly**
Dear Mr. Henshaw
Ellen Tebbits
Emily's Runaway Imagination
Henry and Ribsy
Henry and the Paper Route
Henry Huggins
Muggie Maggie
Otis Spofford

**Cole, Joanna**
The Magic School Bus books

**Dahl, Roald**
The BFG
Charlie and the Chocolate
Factory
Charlie and the Great Glass
Elevator
Fantastic Mr. Fox
George's Marvelous Medicine
Matilda
Witches

**Danzinger, Paula**
Amber Brown Is Not a Crayon

**Dicamillo, Kate**
Because of Winn-Dixie

**Dixon, Franklin W.**
The Hardy Boys Mysteries

**Doyle, Sir Arthur Conan**
Sherlock Holmes Mysteries

**Estes, Eleanor Ruth**
Hundred Dresses

**Ferguson, Alane**
Cricket and the Crackerbox Kid

**Fitzgerald, John Dennis**
The Great Brain books

**Fitzhugh, Louise**
Harriet the Spy

**Fleischman, Sid**
The Whipping Boy

**Gardiner, John Reynolds**
Stone Fox

**Grove, Vicki**
Good-Bye My Wishing Star

**Hass, E. A.**
Incognito Mosquito books

**Horvath, Polly**
The Trolls

**Howe, Deborah**
Bunnicula

**Keene, Carolyn**
The Nancy Drew Mysteries

**Kingfisher Publications**
1,000 Facts about People
1,000 Facts about Space
1,000 Facts about Wild
Animals
Forest Animals
Polar Animals
Seashore Animals

**Lowry, Lois**
All about Sam
Anastasia Krupnik series

**Money, Walt**
Gentle Ben
Kavik, the Wolf Dog

**Mowat, Farley**
Owls in the Family

**Nixon, Joan Lowery**
Search for the Shadowman

**Paterson, Katherine**
The Bridge to Terabithia

**Paulsen, Gary**
Dunc and Amos Hit the Big
Top
Dunc and the Flaming Ghost
Dunc Breaks the Record
Dunc Gets Tweaked
Hatchet
Escape from Fire Mountain
Legend of Red Horse Cavern
Rodomonte's Revenge
Wild Culpepper Cruise

**Peck, Robert Newton**
Soup

**Peet, Bill**
Bill Peet: An Autobiography

**Rockwell, Thomas**
How to Eat Fried Worms

**Sachar, Louis**
There's a Boy in the Girls'
Bathroom
Sideways Stories from
Wayside School

**Schulz, Charles**
For the Love of Peanuts

**Silverstein, Shel**
Where the Sidewalk Ends

**Sobol, Donald J.**
Encyclopedia Brown series

**Speare, Elizabeth George**
Calico Captive
Sign of the Beaver

**Van Draanen, Wendelin**
Sammy Keyes and the Hotel
Thief

**Warner, Gertrude Chandler**
Boxcar Children books

# What Is Time?

Where does time go?

1   **SPACE:** an area that goes infinitely in all directions.

**TIME:** a definite moment, such as a second, minute, hour, day, month, or year, fixed by a clock or calendar.

2   Time is an idea that humans can neither see nor feel. It is something you measure, but have no control over. To understand time you need to understand space.

3   Space is where you move. You can move forward and backward, left and right, up and down. Because of this, we say space has three **dimensions**. Imagine yourself playing hopscotch. You move forward, pick up your beanbag, and then hop back home. You have passed through all three dimensions. The **first dimension** is straight forward and back, or a *line (spaces 1, 4, 7, 10 on the hopscotch court)*. The **second dimension** is left and right, or a *plane (spaces 2 and 3, 5 and 6, 8 and 9)*. Finally, the **third dimension** is up and down *(picking up the beanbag)*. We think of the third dimension as being a *cube* because a cube has length, width, and height.

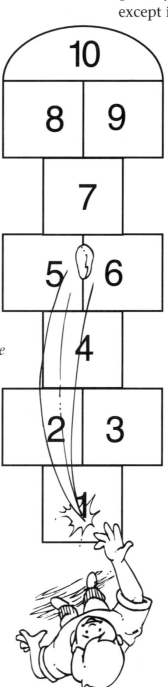

4   Space is a place where you can go backwards. Now, think about the **time** you spent playing hopscotch. Can you go backwards in time? Time that has already been spent or gone by is called the **past**. It doesn't really exist, except in your memories. Time that still needs to happen is called the **future.** This also doesn't exist, except in your mind. The **present** is time that is happening at this very moment. The words you just read are now in the past. The words you will read are in the future. But the word you are reading now is in the present.

5   Scientists call time the **fourth dimension**. By now, your head is probably getting achy trying to understand these dimensions and what this all means. Don't worry! Albert Einstein, an extraordinary genius who lived during the twentieth century, struggled for years before he developed an idea, or theory, that deals with time and space. It is called the **Theory of Relativity.** Einstein's theory has helped other scientists understand that *time travel* might be possible in the future

6   For now, the important fact to understand is that time goes by. Except for the very moment that something is happening, time is always in the past or the future.

*Time stands still for no one.*

www.summerbridgeactivities.com   **Reading Connection—Grade 4—RBP0199**

## Comprehension

Write a **T** before the sentences that are true.
Write an **F** before the sentences that are false.

1. ____ Einstein lived in the 21st century.

2. ____ Space has three dimensions.

3. ____ Time is the fourth dimension.

4. ____ Answering question #1 is in the past, and question #5 is in the future.

5. ____ Humans can measure and control time.

6. Check the sentence that best states the main idea of "What Is Time?"
   ____ Einstein was a genius.
   ____ Time is a definite moment, fixed by a clock or calendar.
   ____ There are many dimensions in time and space.

7. What does "time stands still for no one" mean? _____
   _____
   _____

## Vocabulary Development

An **antonym** is a word that means the opposite of another word. Write an antonym for each of the following words.

1. future _____

2. backward _____

3. left _____

4. up _____

Circle the best meaning for each word.

5. **genius**
   smart          athletic          wealthy

6. **dimension**
   score          measurement          weight

7. **extraordinary**
   common          above normal          average

## Reading Skills

Do you remember that **verbs** are action words? The **tense** of a verb shows time. A verb can be written in **past**, **present**, or **future tense**.

Write the following verbs in past and present tense.

| Future | Past | Present |
|--------|------|---------|
| 1. will run | ran | run |
| 2. will eat | _____ | _____ |
| 3. will jump | _____ | _____ |
| 4. will sleep | _____ | _____ |
| 5. will read | _____ | _____ |
| 6. will speak | _____ | _____ |
| 7. will dance | _____ | _____ |
| 8. will walk | _____ | _____ |
| 9. will jog | _____ | _____ |

## Study Skills

The ability to create an **outline** is a useful study skill to master. An outline shows the important facts learned from written stories.

Use facts from paragraphs 3 and 5 to complete Part I. Use facts from paragraph 5 to complete Part II.

I. The first four dimensions are
   A. the first—a line
   B. the second—a plane
   C. _____
   D. _____

II. Albert Einstein, a 20th-century scientist,
   A. was an extraordinary genius
   B. _____
   C. _____

# The Sunny Side of Time
Would you like to play Midnight Baseball?

## Earth's Rotation

1   The earth spins on an imaginary pole called an **axis**. This pole runs through the South Pole and comes out the North Pole. As the earth rotates around, light falls on it as it faces the sun. Darkness comes to the parts of Earth that are facing away from the sun. Light to darkness, then back to light, this pattern repeats itself every 24 hours.

## The Midnight Sun

2   At the North Pole, during the months of December and January there is complete darkness. In June and July there is endless sunlight. Living in the very northern part of our world, in places such as Alaska, Greenland, or Canada, can be difficult for people.

3   Humans have an invisible "living clock" in their brain. Scientists who study the brain haven't yet found the clock's location. This clock becomes confused when there's not a steady amount of light, then darkness each day. When it is dark, the brain tells the body to sleep. When it's light, the brain tells the body to wake up. What would your body want to do if it was dark outside for two whole months?

If you're planning a summer vacation in Alaska, be sure to play a game of Midnight Baseball. That's right! The sun is bright enough at midnight that you'll need to shade your eyes to catch a fly ball.

## Upside Down

4   If you lived south of the equator, in countries such as Chile or New Zealand, you'd have summer when the United States is having winter. Summer for those countries occurs when the South Pole is pointing towards the sun. Of course, that makes the North Pole very dark for several months. Then, the opposite happens as Earth continues its orbit around the sun. The South Pole gets dark, and the North Pole gets sunny.

Many animals and plants have built-in clocks. For example, a plant called a four-o'clock opens its petals at about four in the afternoon. The Canadian goose flies south in the winter. Grizzly bears come out of hibernation in the spring.

what time is it ?!?

## World Time Zones

5   The world is divided into 24 **time zones**. Each time zone matches one hour of time during the day. If you travel east from one time zone to another you lose one hour. Suppose you are in Chicago and you call your grandmother in New York City. She lives one time zone away from you. It is 8:00 P.M. *your time*; what time is it in New York City?

© RBP Books     www.summerbridgeactivities.com     Reading Connection—Grade 4—RBP0199

## Comprehension

1. Where is the human "living clock"?
   _____

2. If you lived in Chile and spent your summer vacation in Alaska, what kind of weather should you expect there?
   _____

3. What kind of pole runs through the middle of Earth? _____

4. A Canadian goose flies south. What is the cause? _____

5. Darkness comes to San Francisco. What is the cause? _____

6. The world is divided into 24 time zones. Why? _____

7. Name two countries that are in the northernmost part of the world.
   _____
   _____

## Vocabulary Development

1. Write the two other directions that go with *northern* and *southern*. _____
   _____

**Synonyms** are words that have similar meanings. Match the number of the word with its synonym.

2. orbit          ____ researcher
3. rotates        ____ pole
4. confused       ____ model
5. faces          ____ spins
6. shade          ____ total
7. pattern        ____ meets
8. scientist      ____ hide
9. complete       ____ path
10. axis          ____ muddled

## Reading Skills

1. If the suffix **-less** means "without," what does *endless* mean?
   _____

2. What two words make up the compound word *afternoon*?
   _____

3. What does *afternoon* mean?
   _____

Write the plurals of the following words.

4. country    _____
5. goose      _____
6. mouse      _____
7. child      _____
8. moose      _____

## Study Skills

Study the poster. Answer the questions below.

---
**Midnight Baseball League**
Sign up for Midnight Baseball teams begins April 31st at the Nome City Hall.
- boy/girl teams through age 12
- men's 13–18 years
- women's 13–18 years
- cost: $45.00 for the season. Includes shirt and snacks.

Sign up closes May 31, 2004.
---

1. Susan and Bob, two 15-year-olds, want to play on the same team. Can they? Why or why not?_____
   _____

2. There is an error in the first sentence. What is it? _____
   _____

3. When is the last day to sign up? _____
   _____

# A Poet of Sun and Stars
Do you know this famous Scot?

1  Robert Lewis (he later changed the spelling to Louis) Stevenson was born on November 13, 1950, in Edinburgh, Scotland. He grew up in a wealthy family and received an excellent education from private tutors. His father was an engineer who designed magnificent lighthouses along the rocky coastline of Scotland. Robert knew his father wanted him to become an engineer, too. But Robert had a different idea.

2  By the time Robert was seventeen he had decided to become a writer. Luckily for him, he liked to travel. Travel books had recently become the rage in Europe. By writing for travel magazines he was able to have the best of what he loved. He could write and get paid by a publisher to travel to wonderful places!

3  At first, Robert Louis Stevenson wrote for adults. Then, in 1881 he was on vacation along the shores of Scotland with his family. They had the misfortune of rainy weather the entire time. While cooped up in a house with teenagers, he began his tale of *Treasure Island*. When this book sold out at stores all over Great Britain, Robert knew he should write for children.

4  Stevenson spent years traveling through Europe and as far away as California. His travels made him aware of weather, time, and the objects in the sky. These are subjects in many of his children's stories and poems.

## Time to Rise

A birdie with a yellow bill

Hopped upon the window sill

Cocked his shining eye and said:

"Ain't you 'shamed, you sleepy-head?"

## The Sun's Travels

The sun is not-a-bed when I

At night upon my pillow lie;

Still round the earth his way he takes,

And morning after morning makes.


While here at home, in shining day,

We round the sunny garden play,

Each little Indian sleepy-head

Is being kissed and put to bed.


And when at eve I rise from tea,

Day dawns beyond the Atlantic Sea,

And all the children in the West

Are getting up and being dressed.

Engraved on Robert Louis Stevenson's tombstone is the following poem:

**Under the wide and starry sky**

**Dig my grave and let me lie...**

© RBP Books     www.summerbridgeactivities.com     Reading Connection—Grade 4—RBP0199

## Comprehension

1. In the poem "The Sun's Travels" Stevenson wrote "Each little Indian." What country was he writing about?

   _____

2. Circle Stevenson's nationality.
   Scottish        British        Irish

3. Use your own words to describe what "cooped up in a house" means.

   _____

   _____

   _____

4. Describe the coast of Scotland.

   _____

5. In paragraph 1 the author wrote two opinions. Find one and write it below.

   _____

   _____

## Vocabulary Development

In each row circle the word that does **not** belong.

1. publisher     author      writer      pencil

2. Scotland      Germany     Ireland     Britain

3. newspaper     magazine    pen         journal

4. sunrise       morning     sunset      dawn

5. tutor         playmate    teacher     instructor

6. craze         fad         rage        calm

**Antonyms** are words with opposite meanings. Write an **antonym** for the following words:

7. days          _____

8. wonderful     _____

9. best          _____

10. wealthy      _____

## Reading Skills

The prefix **mis-** means "bad" or "badly." For example, *misuse* means to "use something in a bad or wrong way." Write the meaning of the words below.

1. misfortune      _____

2. misinformed     _____

3. misbehave       _____

4. mislead         _____

5. mishandle       _____

Write the two words that form the **compound words** found in the paragraph shown in parentheses.

6. (1) _____ and _____

7. (1) _____ and _____

8. (1) _____ and _____

## Study Skills

Complete the following outline. Use facts from paragraph 1 to complete Part I. Use facts from paragraph 2 to complete Part II and facts from paragraph 3 to complete Part III.

I. Stevenson's Early Life

   A. Born November 13, 1850

   B. _____

   C. _____

II. Stevenson the Writer

   A. _____

   B. _____

   C. _____

III. Later Writing Days

   A. _____

   B. _____

   C. _____

**Reading Connection—Grade 4—RBP0199**          www.summerbridgeactivities.com          ©RBP Books

# Days of the Week

### Anonymous

**Monday's** child is fair of face,

**Tuesday's** child is full of grace,

**Wednesday's** child is full of woe,

**Thursday's** child has far to go,

**Friday's** child is loving and giving,

**Saturday's** child works hard for a living,

But the child that is born on **Sunday**
is blithe and bonny and good and gay.

1   No one seems to agree on the origin of the seven-day week. Most astronomers believe that the Babylonians were the first to break the year up into months. At some point it became important to divide the year into smaller "chunks." Around 1600 B.C. a new period of time was created. It was longer than a day, but less than a month. This was called the **week**.

2   **Seven** days x **4** weeks = **28** days. This is almost as long as a lunar month. A lunar month is how long it takes our moon to orbit the earth. A lunar month is $29\frac{1}{2}$ days. One reason a week is seven days long is because four seven-day weeks is close to a lunar month.

3   Different cultures have had different names for the days of the week. This is not true for the months of the year. Names for the months are remarkably close in *many* languages.

4   In ancient times, people throughout the world could see seven "planets" in the sky without a telescope. They were the sun, moon, Mars, Mercury, Jupiter, Venus, and Saturn. (No one studied the sky with a telescope until Galileo in the sixteenth century. Until then, people thought the sun was a planet.)

5   Many languages connect each day of the week with one of these seven planets. In English you can find planet names in *Monday*, *Saturday*, and *Sunday*. The other four days have been substituted with the names of Scandinavian gods. (Scandinavia is the area that includes the countries of Denmark, Norway, Sweden, and Finland.)

| English | French | Planet |
|---|---|---|
| Monday | lundi | Moon |
| Tuesday | mardi | Mars |
| Wednesday | mercredi | Mercury |
| Thursday | jeudi | Jupiter |
| Friday | vendredi | Venus |
| Saturday | samedi | Saturn |
| Sunday | dimanche | Sun |

6   Countries belonging to the United Nations have agreed that Monday is the first day of the week. While many countries have made Monday the first day of the week, the Jewish and Christian calendars start on Sunday. To make things more complicated, most Christians make Sunday their day of rest and worship. Jews attend their temples on Saturday. The Muslims' holy book, the Koran, calls Friday a holy day or the "king of days."

## Comprehension

1. Write the sentence from "The Days of the Week" that tells when people began to use instruments to look at the sky.

   _____

   _____

Answer each question with a word or group of words.

2. What is French for *Thursday*? _____

3. What are the names of the "planets" that could be seen without a telescope?

   _____

   _____

4. What do Muslims call their holy book?

   _____

5. What day does the United Nations call the first day of the week?_____

6. Describe the child born on Friday.

   _____

7. If you know that a **synonym** for *fair* is *milky* or *blond* and that Monday is named after the moon, why did the author of the poem write "Monday's child is fair of face"? _____

   _____

## Vocabulary Development

Write the letter of the correct definition in front of each word.

1. ____ bonny       A. bright; lively

2. ____ grace       B. the first

3. ____ gay       C. attractive

4. ____ culture       D. a person who studies objects in the sky

5. ____ astronomer       E. a civilization

6. ____ original       F. having charm

## Reading Skills

1. Find the compound word in the poem.

   _____

Find the two compound words in paragraph 4.

2. _____

3. _____

An **adjective** is a word that is used to describe a noun. A **suffix** can be added to the end of an adjective to change its meaning. The suffix **-er** added to an adjective lets the writer make comparisons. For example, when **-er** is added to *dark*, the reader knows something has become *more dark*. Write the meaning of the words below.

4. smaller _____

5. greater _____

## Study Skills

Complete the following outline. Use the facts in paragraph 1 to complete Part I. Use facts from paragraphs 3 and 4 to complete Part II.

  I. Months and days

    A. Babylonians separate years into months.

    B. _____

   _____

   _____

  II. Names of days

    A. Ancient people named days after planets.

    B._____

   _____

   _____

# What's in a Name?

Why is Monday called Monday?

## Moon-day

1   *Monday* is named after the moon. The moon was easy to see in both day and night skies, so early civilizations based their calendars on the moon's orbit around Earth. The Jewish and Islamic calendars are still based on the moon's cycle.

2   Our word *moon* comes from the ancient Saxon word *monandaeg* (*mow-nan-dag*). Saxons were fierce warriors living in an area of Germany. They invaded England in the fifth and sixth centuries. Other countries in Europe use the Latin word for moon, *luna*, as the base word for their word for *Monday*. For example, the French word for Monday is *lundi*. *Luna* is used in English as the base for the word *lunacy*. People used to think the moon had something to do with insanity.

3   "Feeling blue" means to feel sad. Have you ever felt blue on Monday as you head off to school? Don't worry, you're not the only one having this feeling. In many cultures Monday is called **the blue day**. It was thought to be the day people went mad. The Babylonian moon god, Sin, is a wise old man who wears an enormous blue turban and has a long, flowing blue beard.

4   An old tradition in Scotland was to bow to the new moon each month and jingle money in your pocket. This was a superstition to help keep the "blues" away.

## Tues-day

5   Mars, the Roman god of war, was the father of Romulus and Remus. These were the mythical twins who started the city of Rome. A bad-tempered god, Mars loved to pick a fight. The Romans, who had huge armies, worshiped him on Tuesdays. In Italian the word for Tuesday is *martedi*.

6   The word *Tuesday* was brought to England by invading tribes, including the Saxons. These people called Tuesday *tiwesdaeg* (*tee-wahz-dag*) after their god of war, Tiw. A legend says a gigantic wolf named Fenrir bit off Tiw's left hand. This allowed Tiw to capture the wolf's courageous powers.

7   **Runes** are ancient symbols that were used for writing messages and telling fortunes. They were also associated with magic and good luck. The Rune of Tiw was said to protect sailors, the disabled, and the left-handed. Tiw wore a bright red cloak at the start of each battle. Tuesday, Tiw's day, was a day to begin fights, offer dares, and find courage.

www.summerbridgeactivities.com   Reading Connection—Grade 4—RBP0199

## Comprehension

1. A **summary** includes the most important facts about the subject of a paragraph or story. For example, a summary of paragraph 1 could be "Monday is named after the moon." Underline the best summary for paragraph 7 below.

   **a.** Tuesday is a day to begin battles.

   **b.** Runes are ancient symbols used to write messages and protect people.

   **c.** Tiw's color is bright red like Mars.

Answer the following in complete sentences.

2. What did the Scots do to keep from feeling sad?_____

   _____

   _____

3. What does "find courage" mean in paragraph 7? _____

   _____

   _____

## Vocabulary Development

Write the word found in the paragraph in parentheses that best fits the definition.

1. ancient people from the countries of Syria, Iraq, and Saudi Arabia (3)

   _____

2. an untrue idea (4)_____

3. imaginary (5) _____

4. head covering (3) _____

5. honor, adore (5) _____

6. a myth or tale; fiction (6)_____

7. to clang something together (4)

   _____

## Reading Skills

**Adjectives** are words that describe nouns. They make stories more interesting to read. Write the adjective or adjectives found in the paragraph in parentheses that describes the noun. For example, in paragraph 5 the adjective *mythical* describes the noun *twins*.

1. man (3)_____ and _____

2. Saxon (2)_____

3. armies (5) _____

4. wolf (6) _____

5. civilizations (1) _____

6. symbols (7)_____

7. turban (3) _____ and _____

Write the **base word** for the words below.

8. countries _____

9. courageous _____

## Study Skills

Study the newspaper weather forecast below; then answer the questions.

---

**Weather for Stornoway, Scotland**
- Blue skies on Monday
- Cool with temperatures around 10° C
- Thunderstorms Tuesday morning followed by sunny skies
- Flaming red sunsets expected Tuesday night

---

1. What day will have red sunsets?

   _____

2. Is the temperature reported in Fahrenheit or Celsius?_____

3. What is the name of the country where Stornoway is located? _____

# What's in a Name? (continued)

Which day is named for the Norse god of thunder?

## Wednes-day

1   The foreign tribes who came to England around 400–600 A.D. called their most powerful god Odin (*Oh-dean*). He was also called Woden, and it is easy to see where *Woden's Day,* or *Wednesday,* came from.

2   Odin was a fierce hunter, but he loved life. It was said that he brought poetry to the people of Earth. Marigolds, which were used to heal wounds in ancient times, grew wherever Odin's feet touched the ground. For reasons unknown Woden's rune is blank.

3   The Romans named the third day of the week after the planet Mercury. In Latin, *mercari* means "to trade," and the Romans were some of the finest traders, or *merchants*, of all time.

## Thurs-day

4   In Rome, the fourth day of the week was named after Jupiter, who was also called Jove. The Greeks called him Zeus. The strongest god of all, he was king of the skies and mountain-tops. Strong, long-living oaks grew where his thunderbolt struck the earth. *Thursday* in French is *jeudi*.

5   The Norwegian god of thunder was Thor. Carrying a mighty hammer, Thor rode across the sky in a golden chariot protecting humans against giant serpents that lived on the tops of towering mountains. Whenever Thor passed overhead lightning soon followed.

## Fri-day

6   Freya (*Free-yah*) was the goddess of life, health, and love. Our fifth day, Friday, is named for her. She lived in the branches of the beautiful elder tree, and would place spells on anyone, except musicians, who cut wood from her home. The youngest of village girls were trained to harvest the elder tree's bark for making black dye. Its leaves were used for green dye, and its berries for a deep purple dye. Freya's rune was carried close to the heart to bring the wearer peace and love.

7   For the Romans this day was named after the planet Venus. Friday is called *venerdi* in Italian. Venus is often seen as the bright "star" near our moon or at dusk along the western horizon. If you rise early in the morning, before dawn, you can see its beautiful glow in the east.

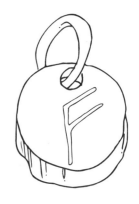

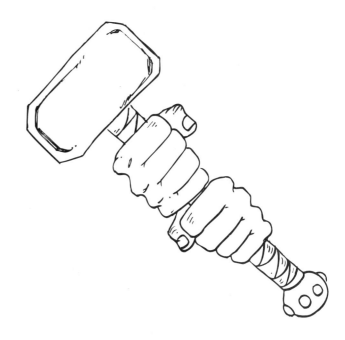

© RBP Books    www.summerbridgeactivities.com    Reading Connection—Grade 4—RBP0199

## Comprehension

Answer these questions in complete sentences.

1. Why do you think the word for Roman traders was *merchant*? _____
_____
_____

2. In paragraph 7 the author calls Venus a "star." What is a star? Use a dictionary if necessary. _____
_____
_____

3. When you see Venus why should you **not** call it a star? _____
_____

4. Write one comparison between Odin and Thor. Use the word *while* in your sentence.
_____
_____

## Vocabulary Development

Write the number of the word that matches the definition.

| Word | Definition |
|------|-----------|
| 1. fierce | ____ lightning |
| 2. harvest | ____ a snake |
| 3. marigold | ____ from the country of Norway |
| 4. thunderbolt | ____ a two-wheeled vehicle used for war or racing |
| 5. serpent | ____ a golden yellow flower |
| 6. chariot | ____ to pick or gather |
| 7. Norwegian | ____ intense, violent |
| 8. blank | ____ from another country |
| 9. foreign | ____ an empty space |

## Reading Skills

Verbs are "doing words." **Action verbs** are words that show some form of movement or action. Circle the action verbs in the sentences below.

1. The Romans named the third day of the week after Mercury.

2. Freya would place spells on people.

3. The thunderbolt struck the earth.

4. Odin's feet touched the ground.

5. Venus rises in the west.

6. The girls harvested purple berries.

7. Giant serpents lived on the mountains.

8. Foreign tribes came to England.

9. Thor passed overhead throwing lightning to the earth.

10. The man carried the rune close to his heart.

## Study Skills

Words can be divided into **syllables**, or word parts. At the end of a line of writing you should only break a word at the end of a syllable. Listening to a word's syllables will also improve your spelling. Separate the following words into their syllables.

| | | |
|------|------|------|
| 1. morning | morn | ing |
| 2. unknown | _____ | |
| 3. purple | _____ | |
| 4. marigold | _____ | |
| 5. merchants | _____ | |
| 6. planet | _____ | |
| 7. Jupiter | _____ | |
| 8. thunderbolt | _____ | |
| 9. Thursday | _____ | |
| 10. ancient | _____ | |

Reading Connection—Grade 4—RBP0199     www.summerbridgeactivities.com     ©RBP Books

# The Weekend
What is your favorite day of the week?

## Satur-day

1   The sixth and seventh days of the week make up the week's end. Many children in the world go to school on Saturdays for a half-day. However, in the United States Saturday is usually a day for sports, play, and shopping.

2   Saturday was named after the planet Saturn. The god Saturn was two-faced, bringing both harm and good everywhere he went. Saturn brought bad luck and death, but he also gave gifts of strength and understanding. The ancient ones gratefully accepted these favors, especially when they were dying.

3   Saturn was known as Old Father Time by some. In fact, the Greeks called Saturn *Cronus*, which means "time." Cronus roamed the earth during the week between what is now Christmas and New Year's Eve. He used his scythe, which is a sharp curved blade, to kill the old year so it could be reborn at midnight on December 31.

4   Saturn's favorite flower was *monkshood*. The ancient Greeks considered this flower to be a symbol of evil. Hidden within its leaves, roots, and velvety purple flowers was a deadly poison. When any part of the plant enters the human body, it causes the heart to beat slower and slower until finally, death comes.

## Sun-day

5   Sunday, or Sun's Day, is the seventh and last day of the week. Its name comes from the German word *Sonntag* (*sown-tag*).

6   The sun is so important to living things that every culture *since the beginning of time* has found a way to honor it. If the sun was somehow extinguished, life would come to an end. Over 3,500 years ago, primitive people painted and carved pictures of the sun in caves. This may have been done as a written prayer to bring the sun back from its long winter sleep.

7   In 321 A.D. Constantine the Great, the first Christian emperor of Rome, ordered that Sunday be a day of rest for all Christians. To work on Sunday was a grave sin. A story from Ireland tells of a farmer who went to plow his fields instead of going to church on Sunday. Within minutes the ground opened up and swallowed the poor man. He was never seen again.

8   The sunflower is probably the plant most of us associate with the sun. Its cheery, round face always looks south so it can follow the sun's path across the sky. That is, of course, if the flower is in the northern hemisphere.

## Comprehension

Write T before the sentences that are true. Write F before the sentences that are false.

**1.** ____ The sunflower is Saturn's favorite flower.

**2.** ____ The Greek word *cronus* means "time."

**3.** ____ Monkshood is a deadly purple flower.

**4.** ____ People painted pictures of the sun in caves hundreds of years ago.

**5.** ____ Human life can exist on Earth without the sun.

**6.** Write a **comparison** of the two faces of Saturn. Remember, in a comparison you tell how two things are alike *or* different.

_____

_____

_____

**7.** Check the sentence that is the best main idea for the story.
____ Saturn was a fearful god.
____ Living things need the sun.
____ The weekend days are Saturday and Sunday.

**8.** In the southern hemisphere, which direction would a sunflower's head face?

_____

_____

## Vocabulary Development

In each row, circle the word that **doesn't** belong.

| | | | |
|---|---|---|---|
| **1.** poison | medicine | venom | germ |
| **2.** young | old | ancient | aged |
| **3.** attractive | stunning | plain | pretty |
| **4.** primitive | modern | original | ancient |
| **5.** soft | smooth | velvety | rough |
| **6.** busy | entertain | occupy | bore |
| **7.** planet | hoe | dig | plow |
| **8.** grave | dangerous | serious | silly |

## Reading Skills

Often when reading you come across words that you don't know. When you don't know the meaning of a word you have three choices:

1. You can look up the word in a dictionary.

2. You can ask someone the meaning of the word.

3. You can continue reading and see if the definition of the word appears in the paragraph. This is called a **context clue**.

Note: Don't skip words you don't know. This will get in the way of comprehension.

Find the definition of the words below. The context clues will be in the paragraph in parentheses.

**1.** scythe (3) _____

**2.** monkshood (4) _____

**3.** two-faced (2) _____

## Study Skills

Use the dictionary entry below to answer the questions.

> **favor** \fā-vər\ n 1. a helpful act 2. a small gift given to a party guest

**1.** Underline the sentence in which *favor* has the same meaning as definition 1.
• Saturn was in favor of kicking Thor out of the Heavens.
• The sun did the earth a favor by warming her cold mountains.

**2.** Write a sentence that uses *favor* meaning "a small gift." _____

_____

_____

**3.** Is *favor* used here as a noun or a verb? ____

_____

# Months of the Year

Why are there 365 days in a year?

1   There are roughly twelve **lunar months** in a year. A lunar month is the time it takes the moon to rotate around the earth. During that time the moon changes from a new moon ☽, to a full moon ○, to an old moon ☾. Finally, it disappears for a whole night before it begins the process all over again.

2   People who used calendars based on the moon slowly began to realize that *time was out of whack*. A little over 2,000 years ago the Romans realized that celebrations for spring were taking place during the dark days of winter, and farmers were saying their winter prayers while harvesting autumn crops. It was a big mess. Something had to be done!

3   At first the Romans tried to fix this mess by changing the length of the year. The new year could be between 355 and 378 days long. Sometimes they added an extra month. As you might guess, this only made things worse.

4   Finally, after years of studying the stars and planets, a Roman astronomer figured out the problem. The lunar calendar was inaccurate by $1\frac{1}{4}$ days. Sosigenes (*So-see-gee-nez*) was able to estimate that it took the sun 365 days and 6 hours to rotate around the earth. He called this a **solar year**, or sun year. (It took another 1,700 years before everyone agreed that the earth rotated around the sun.)

5   Julius Caesar (*See-zer*), a great Roman leader, put an end to the lunar calendar. On January 1, 45 A.D., the Romans switched to the solar calendar of 365 days. Every four years an extra day was added at the end of February. This was called a **leap year**.

6   This worked for about 1,500 years, but by the sixteenth century the Julian calendar was ten days off. A year is actually 365 days, 5 hours, 48 minutes, and 49.7 seconds long. In 1583 Pope Gregory, along with mathematicians and astronomers, created a new calendar.

7   First, they decided that there would be a leap year in 1600. The next three centennial years would not have a leap year. There was a leap year in 2000, so the next centennial leap year won't be until 2400. Second, Pope Gregory decided to change October 5, 1583, to October 15, 1583. This made a lot of people mad. There were even riots in big cities because people thought their lives were being shortened by 10 days. As fears about the Gregorian calendar calmed, it was slowly adopted throughout the Christian world. Now the calendar is only one day off every 20,000 years.

8   **Here is an old rhyme children used to help memorize the number of days in each month:**

> Thirty days has September,
>
> April, and June, and November;
>
> All the rest have thirty-one,
>
> except February alone,
>
> which has twenty-eight
>
> and twenty-nine in each leap year.

© RBP Books    www.summerbridgeactivities.com    Reading Connection—Grade 4—RBP0199

# Comprehension

Circle the best answer to the questions below.

1. What was the name of the astronomer who estimated the length of the solar year?
   Caesar          Sosigenes          Gregory

2. A lunar month is how long?
   ____ the time it takes the moon to rotate around the sun
   ____ the time it takes for the moon to rotate around Earth

3. How many years are in a century?
   10               100                1,000

4. What did Pope Gregory do that made people think their lives were being shortened by ten days? (paragraph 7)_____
   _____
   _____

5. What does an astronomer do? (paragraph 4)
   _____

# Vocabulary Development

An **antonym** is a word that means the opposite of another word. Write an antonym for each word below.

1. rough       _____
2. problem     _____
3. winter      _____
4. spring      _____
5. mad         _____
6. harvest     _____
7. huge        _____
8. inaccurate  _____
9. calm        _____

A **thesaurus** is a good reference book for this activity. A thesaurus lists synonyms and antonyms. Look up *riot* and see what you find!

10. riot _____

# Reading Skills

A **context clue** is when the meaning of a word can be found within the paragraphs being read. For example, in the second sentence of paragraph 1 you find the context clue for the meaning of *lunar month*.

Be the detective and find the context clues that tell you the meanings of the words below. The clue will be in the paragraph in the parentheses.

1. solar year (4) _____
   _____

2. Julian calendar (5) _____
   _____

3. Gregorian calendar (7) _____
   _____

4. out of whack (2) _____
   _____

# Study Skills

A **timeline** is a useful tool when doing research for a class report or studying for a test. It puts dates and events in order so you can better understand how time passed. Study the timeline below and answer the questions.

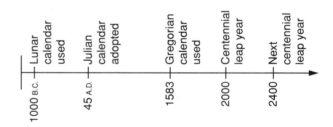

1. When did Julius Caesar introduce his calendar?_____

2. When was the last centennial leap year?
   _____

3. What year were you born?_____

4. How old would you need to be to celebrate the next centennial leap year? _____

Monday                                    April 11, 1955

# President Says No! to World Calendar

### By Samantha Warts
### *The Zipper Press*

1   NEW YORK CITY – The United Nations met yesterday to discuss the idea of a World Calendar. President Eisenhower's close friend, Henry Cabot Lodge, told the gathering of nations that the United States was against the plan.

2   He explained that our president, Dwight Eisenhower, felt it would be unfair to people of Jewish or Muslim faiths. These religions use a calendar based on the orbit of the moon around Earth. The World Calendar, however, is based on the orbit of the earth around the sun.

> The United Nations is a large "club" of countries. Its goal is to improve friendship and peace among nations. During World War II, it was set up by the United States, Great Britain, the Soviet Union, France, and many other countries.
>
> Now, people from nations all over the world come together in New York City. The U.N. hopes better communication between countries will lead to lasting peace.

3   Elizabeth Achelis designed the World Calendar 25 years ago. Her calendar is broken into exactly 52 weeks. Each year would have 364 days instead of the 365 days we have now.

4   Miss Achelis insists that the present calendar, which Pope Gregory III created in 1583, is wrong. In a recent interview with the *New England Post,* she said, "The calendar we use today is over 400 years old. From year to year no one ever seems to know on what day of the week Christmas, New Year's, or the Fourth of July will fall. It divides 365 days into 7-day weeks. The only problem is you can't do that! Pope Gregory's calendar has $365\frac{1}{4}$ days each year. I ask you, how do you have a fourth of a day?"

5   The World Calendar would have a day without a number following every December 30. This day, called Worldsday, would be a holiday throughout the entire world. Also, every four years another day without a number would follow June 30. It would be called Leap Year Day.

6   All holidays would fall on the same day, every year. Christmas would always be on Monday and New Year's on Sunday. Your birthday would always be on Friday if you were born on a Friday.

7   President Eisenhower told reporters last week that the calendar idea bothered him. The president agreed that it would be easier for all nations to have identical timetables, such as the World Calendar. Still, he felt it would be unjust to religions which use a moon calendar to set their holy days. President Eisenhower closed by saying, "I feel no change is needed. Our present calendar is perfectly fine."

## Comprehension

1. Number the events in the order they happened.

   ____ Miss Achelis creates the World Calendar.

   ____ President Eisenhower discusses the World Calendar.

   ____ Samantha Warts writes a news article.

   ____ Henry Cabot Lodge talks to the U.N.

## Vocabulary Development

Find the word in the paragraph shown in parentheses that best fits the given definition.

*Example:* The leader of a country (5).

*Answer:* <u>President</u>

1. A conversation with a news reporter (4)
   _____

2. to talk about something (1)
   _____

3. told the reason for a belief (2)
   _____

4. annoyed, worried (7) _____

5. the same (7) _____

6. following third (4) _____

7. a time schedule (5)_____

8. a vacation (5)_____

9. not fair (7) _____

10. made or created (3) _____

## Reading Skills

Combining two shorter words makes a **compound word**. Find the compound word in each sentence below and write the two words that make the compound.

1. The day following December 30th would be called Worldsday.

   _____ and _____

2. This day would be a holiday throughout the entire world.

   _____ and _____

3. It would be easier for nations to have the same timetable.

   _____ and _____

4. If you were born on a Friday your birthday would always be on Friday.

   _____ and _____

## Study Skills

When reading a newspaper it is possible to gather information from the **headings**. This can be helpful if you are researching a report for history class. Use the heading on the previous page to answer the following questions.

1. What day and date was this news article written? _____

2. Who wrote the article? _____
   _____

3. What newspaper printed the article?
   _____

4. What press does Samantha Warts work for?
   _____

# The Lighter Side of Time

Can you really slow down time?

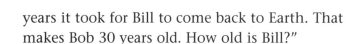

The only reason for time is so that everything doesn't happen at once. —Albert Einstein

1   "I'm going to fail science, Dad," said Conner.

2   "Why do you say that?"

3   "We're having a test on Einstein and his theory on time and space. I just don't understand him!"

4   Dad's face lit up with a huge smile. "Conner, when I was in college everyone in the math department used to say that even Einstein had a hard time understanding Einstein's Theory of Relativity. I learned a way to see what he was talking about, and even if you don't quite get it, it should help. Do you want to hear?"

5   "Sure, Dad. I'll try anything to pass this test."

6   "Imagine twin boys your age. Are you sixteen, yet?"

7   "You know I'm only ten."

8   "That's right! You're so smart I forgot how young you are. Well, anyway, one of the twins, Bob, stays home. The other twin, Bill, hops aboard a spaceship that can travel at the **speed of light**. That's 186,000 miles per second," explained Dad.

9   "Bill flies to Megagope, a planet ten light-years from Earth. Once he gets there, he and the crew turn right around and head back home."

10   "No exploring or anything?" said Conner.

11   "Nope, no exploring. Meanwhile, ten years have passed on Earth while Bill went to Megagope. Then ten more years passed while Bill returned to Earth. How old is Bob now?"

12   "That's easy! Bob was ten years old plus the ten years it took for the spaceship to get to Megagope. That equals 20. Next, add the ten years it took for Bill to come back to Earth. That makes Bob 30 years old. How old is Bill?"

13   "Good question, Conner. This is where you start to understand Einstein's Theory of Relativity. Since Bill traveled at speeds much faster than speeds you can travel on Earth, his body didn't age nearly as much as Bob's. Bill is still ten."

14   "So, let me see if I get this straight. Bill stays ten because he was flying through space *sooo* fast, but Bob gets older by 20 years because he didn't go fast like Bill."

15   "That's right. Time *passes* differently depending on how fast you go. In Bob's case the faster he went, the slower time passed."

16   "That means I could send an apple into space for ten years, then send the apple back to Earth for another ten years, and still be able to have the apple for lunch."

17   "I think you'll pass your test," said Dad.

18   "Awesome!" said Conner.

**It's not that I'm so smart. It's just that I stay with the problems longer. —Albert Einstein**

www.summerbridgeactivities.com
Reading Connection—Grade 4—RBP0199

## Comprehension

1. Number the events in the order they happened in "The Lighter Side of Time."
   ____ Bill, age ten, comes back to Earth.
   ____ Bob, age ten, stays on Earth.
   ____ Bill's spaceship travels for ten light-years to Megagope.
   ____ Bob, Bill's twin, is now 30 years old.

2. Conner is ten and sends an apple into space at the speed of light. The apple travels 15 light-years into space. It turns around and spends another 15 light-years coming back. The apple is only a couple of months old and still edible. How old will Conner be when he has it for lunch?

   _____

3. Write a comparison between Bob and Bill. Use the word *while* in your sentence.

   _____

   _____

## Vocabulary Development

**Homophones** are words that sound the same but have different meanings. Circle the correct homophone for each sentence.

1. The grandfather clock read ten _____ ten.
   
       passed           past

2. Cold filled the deep, dark _____ of space.

       see             sea

3. Einstein, who loved to garden, thought it was fun to plant _____.

       thyme          time

In each row circle the word that does **not** belong.

4. joke    laugh      cry        smile
5. carrot   orange     peach     tangerine
6. huge    awesome   mammoth    large
7. Circle the best definition of *theory*.
       fact            idea             proof

## Reading Skills

Write the **base word** for each of the following:

1. relativity    _____

2. differently    _____

3. studying    _____

4. faster    _____

To make a word **possessive** add **'s** to the end. Make the words below possessive.

5. spaceship    _____

6. apple    _____

7. children    _____

8. Einstein    _____

## Study Skills

Use the facts from paragraph 4 to complete Part I. Then use the facts from paragraph 8 to complete Part II. Finally, use the facts from paragraphs 14 and 15 to complete Part III.

I. Albert Einstein had a theory.

  A. It's hard to understand.

  B. It's called _____

II. Connor's dad explained Einstein's theory using twin boys for an example.

  A. One twin travels at the _____

  _____

  while the other twin stays at home.

  B. The speed of light is _____

  _____

III. Time is not always the same.

  A. Time changes depending on

  _____

  B. The faster you go the _____

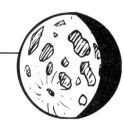

# It's a Silly, Silly Time

Do you know any "nonsense" songs?

Many stories, songs, plays, and poems have been written about time. Most of them have known authors, but occasionally you will see the word **anonymous** instead of the author's name. *Anonymous* is a big word for "unknown," "nameless," or "unmentioned." It's important for you to sign and date every piece you write. Otherwise, you may become anonymous.

The next two pieces are by "Anonymous."

## 'Tis Midnight

1  'Tis midnight, and the setting sun
    Is slowly rising in the west;
  The rapid rivers slowly run,
    The frog is on his downy nest.
  The pensive goat and sportive cow
    Hilarious, leap from bough to bough.

**Anonymous**

## The Train Pulled in the Station

2  O, the train pulled in the station,
    The bell was ringing wet;
  The track ran by the depot,
    And I think it's running yet.

3  'Twas midnight on the ocean,
    Not a streetcar was in sight;
  The sun and moon were shining,
    And it rained all day that night.

4  'Twas a summer day in winter,
    And the snow was raining fast;
  As a barefoot boy, with shoes on,
    Stood, sitting on the grass.

5  O, I jumped into the river,
    Just because it had a bed;
  I took a sheet of water
    For to cover up my head.

6  O, the rain makes all things beautiful,
    The flowers and grasses, too;
  If the rain makes all things beautiful,
    Why don't it rain on you?

**An American Folk Song**

© **RBP Books**    www.summerbridgeactivities.com    Reading Connection—Grade 4—RBP0199

## Comprehension

"The Train Pulled in the Station" is a **nonsense**, or silly, poem. In every **stanza**, or group of lines, the writer creates pictures for the reader's mind that can be confusing. Did you have to read some lines more than once?

For each stanza write one thing that doesn't make **sense**. For example, in stanza 1 a train track doesn't run.

1. Stanza 1 _____

2. Stanza 2 _____

3. Stanza 3 _____

4. Stanza 4 _____

5. Stanza 5 _____

Write what you think is the silliest part of "'Tis Midnight." Be sure to tell **why** you think it's silly.

6. _____

_____

_____

## Vocabulary Development

**Homographs** are words that are spelled the same but have different meanings. Check the meaning of the underlined homograph as it is used in the sentence.

1. <u>Dates</u> are often used when making muffins.

____ a kind of fruit

____ a day in a month

2. The holy man went on a <u>fast</u>.

____ swift moving

____ to not eat food for a period of time

3. Cheese <u>ages</u> rapidly.

____ to grow old

____ long periods of time

## Reading Skills

Write the words that make up the **compound words** found in the stanzas in parentheses.

1. (3) _____ and _____.

2. (4) _____ and _____.

The suffix **-less** means "to be without." For example, *nameless* means to be without a name. Write the meaning of each word below.

3. friendless _____

4. homeless _____

5. hopeless _____

6. helpless _____

## Study Skills

This is an entry form for a contest called "The Best Ever Child Poet in America." Fill out the entry form. Then answer the questions below.

```
┌ ─ ─ ─ ─ ─ ─ ─ ─ ─ ─ ─ ─ ─ ─ ┐
  Name _____
            Last          First
  Address _____
              Street
          _____
              City
          _____
            State        Zip code
  School _____
  English Teacher's Name _____
  Birth Date _____
              Day   Month   Year
  Grade in School _____
  Signature _____
└ ─ ─ ─ ─ ─ ─ ─ ─ ─ ─ ─ ─ ─ ─ ┘
```

1. What part of your name do you write first? _____

2. How many lines are used for your address? _____

3. What is written last on the form? _____

# Sun and Water

How did the ancient Egyptians tell time?

## Shadow Clocks

1  The Egyptians and Babylonians were fascinated with the sun and time. One of the earliest clocks was invented in the Middle East about 4,000 years ago. It is called a **shadow clock**. It was a T-shaped piece of wood with a time scale carved on it. As the sun rose into the sky the shadow it cast became longer. After noon, as the day moved toward sunset, the shadow grew shorter.

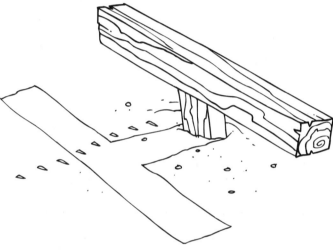

## Water Clocks

2  A most inventive clock for cloudy days or indoor use was the water clock. The **clepsydra** (kelp-sa-dra) had its origins, or beginnings, in Egypt about 1500 B.C. *Clepsydra* is a Greek word that means "water thief." Other night clocks, such as candle and rope clocks, could only be used once. The water clock could be used over and over again.

3  People have built water clocks for three millenniums. Though the clocks were different, one basic rule remained the same. Water constantly dripped from one container through a small hole in its bottom to another. Perhaps the most famous use for this type of clock was in ancient Greece. There, lawyers' speeches were limited by the number of drops that passed through the hole.

4  Egyptian clock makers formed clay pots with a tiny hole in the bottom and carved lines around the side. As water slowly dripped out of one pot into another, it was possible to tell how much time had passed by the changing water level.

5  In museums, you can see ancient water clocks that are glazed in beautiful colors with designs from the night sky. Some water clocks rang brass bells or opened wooden doors to reveal little dancing people.

6  Although sunlight wasn't needed for a water clock to work, it still had several problems. When it became very cold, the water would freeze and not drip at all. When it was very hot the water would evaporate quickly. Eventually, the drip-drip of the water clock was replaced by the tick-tock of the mechanical clock. The first mechanical clock was built in the late fourteenth century.

389 DROPS. TIME IS UP!

© RBP Books          www.summerbridgeactivities.com          Reading Connection—Grade 4—RBP0199

## Comprehension

Write **F** before the sentences that are fact.
Write **O** before the sentences that are opinion.

1. ____ The Egyptians were fascinated with the sun and time.

2. ____ Water clocks were glazed in beautiful colors.

3. ____ *Clepsydra* means "water thief" in Greek.

A **comparison** is when you tell the ways in which two things are alike or different. For example, when comparing a dog and cat you could write, *The cat meows while the dog barks.* Write a comparison between the shadow and the water clocks. Use a complete sentence.

_____

_____

_____

## Vocabulary Development

**Antonyms** are words with opposite meanings. Write an antonym for each word below.

1. fascinated  _____

2. beginning  _____

3. sunlight  _____

4. ancient  _____

5. sunset  _____

Find the word in the paragraph in the parentheses that best fits the definition.

6. creative; original (2) _____

7. uses parts to create a complex tool (6)

   _____

8. one thousand years (3) _____

9. the people and culture of a certain African nation (4) _____

## Reading Skills

Write a **compound word** using two words from each sentence below.

1. At noon each day, the young boy went after a pail of water.

   _____

2. The potter used a small pin to make a hole in the bottom of the bowl.

   _____

3. It is impossible to tell time by using a sundial at night. _____

Complete each sentence below with the correct possessive noun.

4. The _____ clock shop faced an alley.

   Egyptians      Egyptian's      Egyptians's

5. Yesterday all the _____ hands fell off.

   clocks      clock's      clocks'

## Study Skills

Edward was traveling to Cairo, Egypt, to visit the pyramids and the museums. Use his travel schedule below to answer the questions.

| No Bother Airlines | | | |
|---|---|---|---|
| *New York City to Cairo* | | | |
| Date | Flight | Leaves | Arrives |
| April 1 | 1492 | 9:55 A.M. | 10:55 P.M. |
| July 4 | 1776 | 6:32 A.M. | 8:41 P.M. |
| Oct. 12 | 2001 | 10:17 A.M. | 11:59 P.M. |

1. If he wants to travel in the spring, which flight should he take? _____

2. What city will he be leaving from to fly to Cairo? _____

3. Which airline should he call if he wants to book a flight? _____

4. What is the latest flight? _____

# A Sunshiny Shower
Can you make an alarm clock from a candle?

A sunshiny shower won't last a half an hour.
—Anonymous

1   Over time, people have invented many kinds of timekeepers. The shadow and water clock could give a fairly accurate idea of the hour in a day. However, they were not useful for shorter time intervals such as a quarter or half hour.

## Candle Clocks

2   A candle couldn't be used to *find* the time, like a shadow clock could. But it could be used to tell the *passage of time*. In the ninth century, King Alfred the Great said a candle could be marked with slashes to show the passing of quarter hours as it melted. The candles had to be made exactly the same width because fat candles burn slower than skinny ones.

3   Candle clocks were also made with tiny bells embedded in them. When the candle melted down to the bell, it would fall, landing into a tin holding the candle. Now you could use a candle as an alarm clock! These candles were utilized for nearly a thousand years. English soldiers used them on battlefields, keeping them in lanterns to protect them from the wind.

4   From about 500–1600 A.D. the Chinese used incense to tell time. Incense burns at a regular rate (like the drip-drip or tick-tock of other clocks), so it was perfect for measuring time. The clocks were made with differing scents of incense so people could smell when the hour changed!

## Sand Clocks

5   On sailing ships water clocks would spill when the seas were rough, and shadow clocks only worked when there was sun. The pendulum clock was invented in the seventeenth century. It did not need sun, but on a ship the pendulum would crash into the clock's sides. This would stop or break the clock. So sailors used sand clocks to keep time.

6   Sand clocks were called **hourglasses** or **sandglasses**. They were made from two glass bulbs joined by a narrow neck. The clocks were actually filled with powdered eggshell that flowed at a steady rate from the top bulb to the bottom. They worked in any type of weather, day or night.

7   Sailors usually worked four hours at a time. This was called a four-hour **watch**, and four-hour sand clocks were kept aboard ships until about three hundred years ago. Nowadays, you can buy little "three-minute" sand clocks, the time needed to boil an egg.

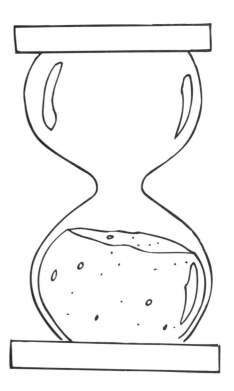

www.summerbridgeactivities.com

## Comprehension

Answer the questions below with complete sentences.

1. Fine, dry sand can be hard to find if you don't live near an ocean. What did people use in their "sand clocks" instead of sand?

   _____

2. Name two things that you could stick into a candle, other than a bell, that would sound "alarms" as the candle melted.

   _____

   _____

3. What caused the pendulum on a shipboard clock to crash into its wooden sides?

   _____

   _____

## Vocabulary Development

An **idiom** is a group of words that has special meaning not easily understood by its parts. For example, *to put up with* means "to tolerate." Write the idiom found in the paragraph in parentheses that matches the meaning.

1. tell time (5) _____

2. during the past (1) _____

Find the word in the paragraph shown in parentheses that **best** fits the description.

3. inserted (3) _____

4. periods; spaces (1)_____

5. spice sticks (4) _____

6. a globe (6)_____

7. a hanging, swinging rod (5)_____

8. on a deck of a ship (7)_____

9. smells; aromas (4) _____

## Reading Skills

**Homographs** are two words that are spelled the same with different meanings. Check the correct meaning for the underlined word.

1. The powerful <u>wind</u> caused the pendulum to smash into the side of its case.

   ____breeze, air current

   ____to turn or bend

2. The child needed to <u>boil</u> the egg for three minutes.

   ____ to become quite angry

   ____ bubble; cook

3. The <u>shadow</u> cast by the stick showed it was after noon.

   ____ to follow or watch

   ____ darkness

4. The clock maker tried to use <u>down</u> instead of sand.

   ____ below; groundward

   ____ new feathers

## Study Skills

A **want ad** is an advertisement placed in a newspaper or magazine asking to buy something. Use the want ad to answer the questions.

---

**WANTED**

Old hourglasses. $1000 for four-hour models. Call Bernie at (811) 555-2134.

---

1. What is Bernie's area code? _____

2. What does Bernie want?_____

   _____

3. How much will Bernie pay for four-hour sand clocks? _____

4. Who is the seller? _____

# The Sandman Cometh

You can build your own hourglass.

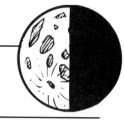

1    Have you ever gotten up in the morning and noticed a gritty substance in the corner of your eyes? For centuries mothers and fathers have tucked their children into bed and told them the Sandman will come to help them sleep. Come morning, the children have grit that needs to be removed from their eyes. Could this be proof that the Sandman had paid a visit?

2    **Here are directions for making your own sand clock. It is always a good idea to read through directions completely before starting any project.**

- a plastic milk or juice carton
- a large, clean glass (a big jam jar works)
- a small nail
- a clock
- enough dry sand to fill the plastic carton half full
- some sheets of newspaper
- a black marker

## Step 1

3    On a warm, sunny day put the plastic carton, the glass jar, and the sand out in the sunlight. Spread the sand on the newspaper. In a few hours all three items should be extremely dry.

## Step 2

4    Use the nail to punch a small hole in the bottom of the plastic carton. Next, fill the carton with sand. You can use a metal funnel to help get the sand in the narrow opening. To make an easy funnel, roll a sheet of newspaper up on the diagonal. If the sand doesn't start running out of the carton, make the hole bigger, a little at a time, until the sand comes out slow and steady.

## Step 3

5    After you get the hole just right, fill the carton half full of sand. Place the carton over the open mouth of the glass jar. If the carton is too wobbly, you probably need a bigger jar.

## Step 4

6    Look at the clock. When ten minutes have passed, use your black marker to draw a line on the glass jar. Write *ten minutes* next to the line. Do this five more times, and you have an **hourglass**. Return the sand to the plastic carton every time you want to measure time.

## Name That Time

Hand out scrap paper and pencils to everyone playing. Explain that in ten minutes they need to write down as many words or sayings as they can think of that have to do with time. Set your sand clock running and say Go! At the end of ten minutes count up who has the most words or sayings. That's the winner. (Use a dictionary or thesaurus if there is a disagreement).

The game can be played alone or in groups.

   www.summerbridgeactivities.com    Reading Connection—Grade 4—RBP0199

Name _____  Date _____

## Comprehension

1. Number the directions in the order in which they are to be done.

   ____ Place plastic carton over jar.

   ____ Dry sand on newspaper.

   ____ Mark jar with black marker.

   ____ Fill carton with sand.

   ____ Punch hole in carton

A **cause** is something that is done. An **effect** is what happens because of what was done.

2. The Sandman sprinkles sand on children's eyes. What effect does this have? _____

   _____

3. In Step 3 the effect is a wobbly carton. What is the cause? _____

   _____

   _____

4. In Step 1 the sand dries out. What is the cause? _____

   _____

## Vocabulary Development

**Synonyms** are words with similar meanings. Write the number of the word on the line next to its synonym.

1. proof        ____ opening

2. challenge    ____ wordbook

3. funnel       ____ shaky

4. thesaurus    ____ evidence

5. grit         ____ waste

6. wobbly       ____ dare

7. scrap        ____ sand

8. mouth        ____ angled tube

## Reading Skills

Write the **base word** for the words below.

1. recyclable   _____

2. centuries    _____

3. sprinkling   _____

4. marker       _____

Write the **possessive** for the words below.

5. everyone     _____

6. substance    _____

7. jar          _____

8. carton       _____

## Study Skills

Number the words in each column in **alphabetical order**.

1. ____ marker      2. ____ cartoon
   ____ maker          ____ carton
   ____ market         ____ canteen

3. ____ jam         4. ____ grass
   ____ jab            ____ glass
   ____ jar            ____ grease

Separate these words into **syllables** to show where the words can be divided at the end of a writing line. Use a dictionary if necessary.

5. recyclable   _____

6. thesaurus    _____

7. dictionary   _____

8. challenge    _____

9. directions   _____

10. plastic     _____

# Tick Tock, You're a Clock

Have you ever had jet lag?

1   All living things have a built-in clock. Scientist call it a **biological clock**. *Bio* means "living." So you have a living clock. Where is this clock? It's inside your body. Unlike your heart, lungs, or kidneys, it doesn't have an exact place. Doctors can't go find your clock if it needs fixing.

2   This biological clock is designed to work with the natural cycles of nature. These cycles include day and night, spring and fall, summer and winter, new moon and full moon. This inner body clock ticked away for thousands of years before humans invented timekeepers.

3   Farmers rose every day with the sun to milk cows and feed chicken. In the winter, a farming family rested longer hours, often going to sleep with the sunset as early as 5:00 P.M. By the time the sun reached its peak on the summer solstice in June, the family was working long hours, using every bit of light late into the evening.

4   The human clock has a cycle that lasts about 25 hours. It is affected by daylight and darkness. People often feel sick when this clock gets disturbed. Studies have shown that students who stay up late and then get up early to go to school have a harder time remembering what was taught in class than students who went to bed earlier.

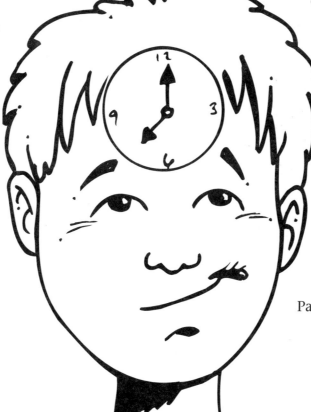

5   Another common problem with a person's clock is something called "jet lag." When you fly on a jet from one time zone to another, your biological clock can get upset. The more time zones you cross, the more likely you are to develop jet lag.

6   For example, if you lived in Kansas City and flew with your parents to New York, you would cross only one time zone. You lose an hour flying east from Kansas to New York. You might feel that you're not quite as sleepy as you normally are at bedtime, but that is not much of a problem.

7   However, if you flew to Paris, you would cross five time zones. Suppose you started your trip at 3:00 P.M. The time in Paris would be 8:00 P.M. Your trip takes ten hours, and you land at the airport in Paris at 6:00 the next morning. The problem is your body clock thinks it's *only one in the morning*. Your inner clock is saying, "Go to sleep! Don't wake up!" Your clock hasn't caught up, it's *lagging* behind.

8   Since your biological clock is set by sunlight it is important when you travel to follow the natural rhythm of the day. That first day in Paris will be hard because you will feel very tired. Luckily, an inner clock isn't too stubborn. In a few days it will be on Parisian time!

© RBP Books    www.summerbridgeactivities.com    Reading Connection—Grade 4—RBP0199

## Comprehension

1. Check the reason the author had for writing this story.
   ____ to tell about jet lag
   ____ to tell about biological clocks
   ____ to encourage young people to get more sleep

2. Check the definition of *jet lag.*
   ____ your biological clock being different from the real time in a place
   ____ something that causes you to get sleepy
   ____ when jets lag behind other jets

3. Where is your "living clock"? _____
   _____
   _____

4. What controls this special clock?_____
   _____
   _____

## Vocabulary Development

1. The summer solstice occurs on the longest day of the year, when the sun is farthest north. Knowing this, what is the definition of the winter solstice?
   _____
   _____

Write the number of the word that matches its **synonym**.

2. upset          ____ natural

3. rhythm         ____ scientist

4. region         ____ cycle

5. normal         ____ zone

6. investigator   ____ disturb

## Reading Skills

1. A **context clue** is a word or group of words that help you understand the meaning of another word. Write the context clue for *lagging* found in paragraph 7.
   _____
   _____

Write the possessive of the following words.

2. Paris     _____

3. jet       _____

4. doctors   _____

5. zone      _____

6. study     _____

## Study Skills

Use the time map below to answer the following questions.

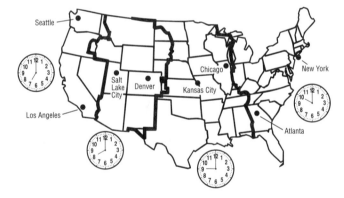

1. If it is 9:00 P.M. in Chicago, what time it in New York? _____

2. How many time zones do you cross when going from Atlanta to Los Angeles?
   _____

3. Is Denver on the same time as Salt Lake City? _____

4. It's 8:00 A.M. in Kansas City. What time is it in Seattle? _____

# Tick Tock, It's a Big Clock

## What is Big Ben really?

1   It's one of the most famous clocks in the world. Millions of people call it Big Ben. The truth is, Big Ben is the 13-ton bell that rings every hour, not the clock itself. Found along the river Thames in London, England, it has been keeping time for more than 150 years.

2   Big Ben was first rung in 1859. The tower in which Big Ben hangs is called St. Stephen's Tower. Others simply call it the Clock Tower. The clock is a pendulum clock. A **pendulum** is a swinging rod with a weight at one end.

3   Most long pendulums in clocks swing from side to side **every second**. A shorter pendulum would swing faster. Inside a pendulum clock are lots of wheels with notches. As the pendulum swings back and forth, it causes the wheels to turn. The notches count the swing of the pendulum. They also make the hands of the clock move.

4   When the clock in St. Stephen's Tower was first built it needed to be rewound every two days. To do this a man had to climb nearly 350 stairs to the top of the belfry. A century ago this was not considered to be a job for a woman.

5   Big Ben is surrounded by several other bells. Four of these bells ring 15 minutes apart, in the musical key of F. On the hour, Big Ben, which chimes the musical note E, plays the Westminster Chimes, adapted from Handel's *Messiah*. Big Ben is said to be named after an extremely large English lord named Sir Benjamin Hall.

> A grandfather clock is a long, narrow clock. Usually it sits on the floor and is tall enough to almost touch the ceiling of a room. Its pendulum swings from side to side 86,400 times a day.

## Big Ben Facts

- The Clock Tower is 320 feet tall.

- It is 200 steps up to the first floor and 350 to the top (belfry).

- The four-quarter bells weigh 1 ton, 1.25 tons, 1.6 tons, and 3.5 tons.

- In 1949, a flock of black birds perched on the clock's minute hand. The clock fell behind $4\frac{1}{2}$ minutes.

- On December 31, 1962, a heavy snowstorm blanketed London. Big Ben rang in the new year ten minutes late because of the heavy ice hanging on its hands.

35

## Comprehension

Circle the correct answer.

1. What is Big Ben?
   a tower      a lord      a bell

2. What is a pendulum?
   a wheel      a rod      a notch

3. Think about how women dressed 150 years ago. Why might climbing 350 stairs be a poor job for a woman in 1859? _____

   _____

4. Why was Big Ben named after an English lord? _____

   _____

5. What do you think makes the ticking sound of a pendulum clock? _____

   _____

## Vocabulary Development

Circle the word that does **not** belong.

1. groove      notch      bump      cut
2. covers      digs      blankets      buries
3. grandfather      son      daughter      uncle
4. basement      tower      belfry      steeple
5. recognized      unknown      popular      famous
6. musical      rhythmic      melodic      noisy
7. commoner      governor      ruler      lord

Circle the definition that best fits the meaning of the underlined word.

8. The painter climbed a <u>rung</u> of the ladder.
   ____ a rounded step
   ____ bells that chimed

9. The boy knew it would be a <u>long</u> time before summer came again.
   ____ a lengthy period
   ____ to wish for; to want

## Reading Skills

1. If the prefix **re-** means to "do again," what does *rewound* mean?

   _____

2. If the suffix **-ly** means "in this way," what does *extremely* mean?

   _____

3. What does *simply* mean? _____

   _____

4. What does *usually* mean? _____

   _____

5. Write the **compound word** found in paragraph 1. _____

## Study Skills

When reading books or papers you often come across numbers. If you are preparing to write a report it is important for you to understand the meaning of those numbers.

Circle the best answer.

1. Which is the largest measurement of weight?
   ounce            ton            pound

2. What two numbers are the same?

   $1\frac{1}{2}$ tons   $1\frac{1}{4}$ tons   1.5 tons   1.5 ounces

3. Read the Big Ben Facts. Now figure out how many years passed between the flock of birds sitting on the minute hand and the heavy snowstorm. _____

   – _____

   Years between _____

4. If a person rested on the first floor of the Clock Tower, how many more steps would he need to climb before he could rewind the bell? _____

# A Time for Limericks

Can you write a limerick?

1   A limerick is a funny poem with five lines. In a limerick, lines 1, 2, and 5 rhyme, and lines 3 and 4 rhyme. We write this rhyme pattern **aabba**. The *a's* stand for lines 1, 2, and 5. The *b's* stand for lines 3 and 4. Where, when, and why people began to write limericks is unknown, but there are many possible answers.

2   One story says that the limerick was a form of song sung by Irish soldiers. They were returning to their hometown of Limerick after fighting a war in France in the early 1700s. Others say limericks appeared in ancient Greek plays centuries before. William Shakespeare even wrote limericks in his plays. *Othello*, *King Lear*, and *Romeo and Juliet* all include limericks.

3   Edward Lear, an English poet, wrote an entire book of limericks. It was called *The Book of Nonsense* and was written in the nineteenth century. At that time, authors of children's books were not listed on the title page. It wasn't until many years later that Lear was recognized for his limericks. The first three limericks below

are by Edward Lear. The last one is by an unknown author.

4   There was an Old Person of Tring

Who embellished his nose with a ring,

He gazed at the moon

Every evening in June,

The ecstatic Old Person in Tring.

5   There was an Old Man who said, "Well!

Will nobody answer the bell?

I have pulled day and night,

Till my hair has grown white,

But nobody will answer this bell!"

6   There was an Old Man on whose nose,

Most birds of the air could repose.

But they all flew away,

At the close of the day,

Which relieved that Old Man and his nose.

7 There was a young lady named Bright,

Who traveled much faster than light.

She started one day

In a relative way,

And returned on the previous night.

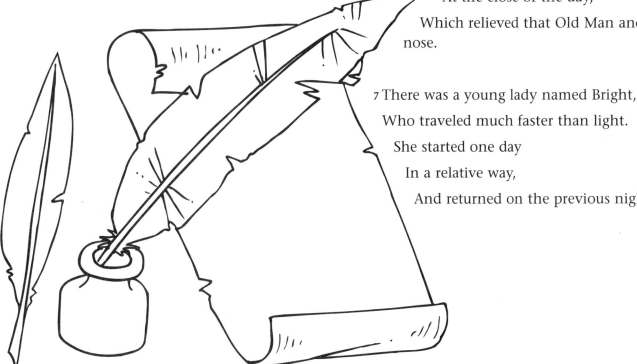

© RBP Books    www.summerbridgeactivities.com    Reading Connection—Grade 4—RBP0199

## Comprehension

**Limericks** are silly, five-lined poems that rhyme in the following pattern: *aabba*.

1. Write a limerick about **time**. Be sure to make it silly!

   _____

   _____

   _____

   _____

   _____

2. Why was the Old Man relieved that the birds flew away at the end of the day?

   _____

   _____

3. (Read paragraph 6 on page 5 before answering this question). What was the author referring to when she wrote "In a relative way" in paragraph 7?

   _____

   _____

## Vocabulary Development

Find the word in the paragraph shown in parentheses that best fits the definition.

1. decorated (4) _____

2. to sleep; rest (6) _____

3. to free from pain
   or embarrassment (6) _____

4. not recognized as a
   fact or person (1) _____

5. a high state of happiness (4) _____

6. identify; know (3) _____

7. a famous English playwright (2) _____

Write the two homophones for *there*:

8. _____

9. _____

## Reading Skills

Write the two words that make up a **compound word** found in the paragraph in the parentheses.

1. (5) _____ and _____.

2. (2) _____ and _____.

Usually, when you want to make a noun plural you add **-s** or **-es** to the end of the word. However, there are nouns that have a different spelling when they become plural. For example, *mouse* becomes *mice*, but *house* does not become *hice*. Write the plural form of each noun below. Use a dictionary if needed.

3. ox _____

4. child _____

5. woman_____

6. man _____

## Study Skills

Use the table of contents below to answer the questions.

**Edward Lear**

1. What is the title of
   the third chapter?_____

2. On what pages could you look
   at pictures about limericks? _____

3. On what pages would you look
   to find out about Lear's early life? _____

4. What chapter tells about
   his writings besides limericks? _____

# The Day Sound Broke

Do you know the story of the first sonic boom?

1  The desert heat rose in shimmering waves as Johnny came to bat. The first ball whizzed past him. "Strike!" shouted his teacher from behind home plate.

2  Sweat dripped down his forehead and stung his eyes. Slowly tapping the dusty base, Johnny tried to buy some time. He needed to calm down. It had been four games since he had had a hit, and the kids in his class were starting to tease him.

3  Squinting to shut out the glaring sun, he watched Bill, his best friend, wind up for another pitch. Without warning the sound rolled across the clear, blue sky. **BOOM!**

4  "Down, boys, down!" Mr. Banks ordered.

5  After a minute or two, the teams rose from the playing field, brushing dirt off their white T-shirts.

6  "What was that?" said Johnny

7  Bill shrugged. "Maybe one of the planes went down."

8  Their small school was near the edge of Rogers Dry Lake in the high desert of southern California. The students knew that super secret aircraft flew over their town every weekday. Young test pilots occasionally could be seen on weekends at the local movie theater or greasy diner. Crashes were frequent at the air base. Johnny's mother often shook her head, saying, "Those poor, poor boys."

9  Test pilots were the elite of the Air Force who flew new models of planes. Often a new plane would have problems. Sometimes these problems ended in a fiery crash that took the pilot's life. Johnny and his friends thought the test pilots were brave to have such a dangerous job.

10  "Holy cow!" said Bill. "Look at that!"

11  As they neared the schoolhouse the boys saw all the windows of the building lying on the ground like fallen snow. Carefully stepping over the sharp glass, they rushed to their classroom where Mr. Banks tuned the radio to the local channel. Static filled the air.

12  Quiet descended on the room as the announcer's voice came over the air. "This is Mike Wilson at Radio KWPX. I have just been in contact with the base at Rogers Dry Lake. I was told that 15 minutes ago, Air Force pilot Charles Yeager broke the sound barrier. He was flying a flaming red, rocket-propelled test plane named *Glamorous Glennis*. The explosion, which has shattered windows across town, is called a sonic boom. Apparently, these booms happen when a plane reaches the speed of sound, which is about 750 miles per hour. On this day, October 14, 1947, America's newest hero is safely back on Earth."

13  As the class began to cheer, Mr. Banks said, "Boys, we'll continue the baseball game tomorrow."

## Comprehension

After reading "The Day Sound Broke" write **T** before the statements that are true and **F** before the statements that are false.

1. ____ Bill was throwing easy pitches to Johnny because they were best friends.
2. ____ Testing new aircraft is a dangerous job.
3. ____ Sonic booms can break glass.
4. ____ The boys cheered because they weren't going to finish their game.

Answer these questions in complete sentences.

5. Why were the aircraft at Rogers Dry Lake super secret? _____ _____

6. Why did Johnny's mom say, "Those poor, poor boys."? _____ _____

## Vocabulary Development

A **simile** is a figure of speech that compares one thing to another using the words *as* or *like*. For example: The bed sheets were as white as a snowy owl.

1. Write the complete simile found in paragraph 11. _____

2. Write the idiom, or saying, in paragraph 12 that means "was heard on the radio." _____

Find the word in the paragraph shown in parentheses that best fits the description.

3. relaxed; unexcited (2) _____
4. the best; the greatest (9) _____
5. fatty (8) _____
6. burning (9) _____
7. came down on (12) _____
8. boundary; wall (12) _____

## Reading Skills

Write the two words that make the **compound word** found in the paragraph in the parentheses.

1. (8) _____ and _____.
2. (8) _____ and _____.
3. (8) _____ and _____.
4. (11) _____ and _____.
5. (11) _____ and _____.
6. (13) _____ and _____.

Write the **base word** for the words below.

7. fallen _____
8. dusty _____
9. whizzed _____
10. tapping _____

## Study Skills

This **bar graph** shows the average temperature at Rogers Dry Lake for the week of October 12–18. Use the graph to answer the questions below.

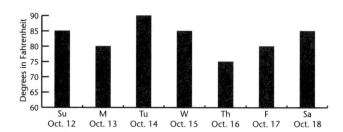

1. Which day was the hottest? _____
2. Which day had the lowest temperature? _____
3. What year were the temperatures recorded? _____
4. What was Tuesday's temperature? _____

# The Handwriting Is on the Wall

What makes you dilly-dally?

1  For thousands of years people have observed the movement of the sun and moon. They have watched the stars and tides, and the daily passing of day and night. So it should come as no surprise that there are many folk sayings about time.

2  A **folk saying** is a short remark people use to make a point. Folk sayings often contain a truth or a bit of wisdom.  Sometimes they are rules for behavior. The next two readings include folk sayings about **time**. Some will be explained, most will not. They have been broken into categories to help you guess their meanings. See if your parents or teacher can help!

## Beginnings

- to jump the gun

3  To **start from scratch** comes from sports. In sports, *scratch* means a line or mark on the ground which is the starting line for a race. The saying "to start from scratch" means to start with the very first step or "at the beginning."

## Endings

- a flash in the pan
- to peter out
- to put the kibosh on
- to the bitter end
- throw in the sponge

The first letter of the Greek alphabet is *alpha*. The last letter is *omega*. Sometimes storytellers will say, **"That's the alpha and omega of it all."** This means the teller of the story is done speaking since she has told both the beginning and the end.

## Sun and Moon

- once in a blue moon
- Indian summer
- dog days of August
- a hunter's moon
- a goose summer

4  **A harvest moon** is the name given to the full moon nearest to September 23. It rises early in the evening and gives additional light for farmers as they harvest their ripe crops.

## Very, Very Slow

- dilly-dally

5  About 150 years ago the saying **a month of Sundays** appeared in the English language. In those days Sundays were spent sitting quietly for many hours in church. At home no games were allowed and certainly no laughter. For a young child the day seemed never-ending. Nowadays, you might say that December feels like *a month of Sundays* while you are waiting for Christmas. In other words, it feels like it will never end!

www.summerbridgeactivities.com   Reading Connection—Grade 4—RBP0199

## Comprehension

Finish each sentence with the best folk saying.

1. If you were making a cake, made a mistake, and needed to begin again, you would say "I need to _____ _____."

2. If you were misbehaving a parent might warn you to stop or else "you would have to do the dinner dishes for a_____ _____."

3. During the summer when it is very hot outside and you see dogs panting to keep cool, you might say, "It's the_____ _____."

4. At a swim meet when a racer dives into the pool too soon, his coach might tell him "to not_____ _____."

5. When your teacher is in a hurry for you to finish your class work he might tell you to "not _____ _____."

## Vocabulary Development

A **thesaurus** is a reference book that contains synonyms and antonyms. In each row below, circle the word that **does not** belong. (Use a thesaurus if needed.)

1. maxim       saying       pledge       proverb
2. folk        tribe        clan         enemy
3. time        moon         globe        satellite
4. notice      overlook     observe      see
5. daystar     sun          orb          planet
6. leader      follower     first        alpha
7. mention     remark       play         comment
8. goose       pig          duck         swan

## Reading Skills

A **base word** is also called a **stem** or **root word**. You add suffixes such as **-less**, **-able**, and **-ous** to the end of base word. Prefixes such as **pre-**, **mis-**, and **un-** are added to the beginning. Prefixes and suffixes change the meaning of the base word. Write the **base** for each word.

1. misbehave       _____
2. friendless      _____
3. preschool       _____
4. famous          _____
5. laughable       _____
6. unhappy         _____
7. mislabel        _____
8. glorious        _____

## Study Skills

At the top of each page in a dictionary you will find two **guide words**. The guide word on the *left* tells you the first word found on the page. The guide word on the *right* tells you the last word on the page. Circle the word that will be found on the page with following guide words.

1. **bowling-brain**
   bread          braid          brawl

2. **golem-gossamer**
   gondola        goal           gourd

3. **liquid-litter**
   lists          live           lion

4. **spoon-spread**
   spoil          sprite         spray

5. **monster-mope**
   morbid         monsoon        moon

6. **flank-flaw**
   flash          flame          flight

7. **work-worst**
   word           world          worth

8. **central-chafe**
   cell           chalet         certain

# More Handwriting Is on the Wall

Have you ever "talked a blue streak"?

## In a Hurry

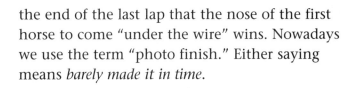

- rarin' to go
- hurry scurry
- lickety-split
- eager beaver
- faster than greased lightning

1   In America we use many expressions brought to our country by British and German immigrants. Many sayings have been changed, or Americanized. One such saying is **to talk a blue streak**, which has roots in several European countries. Lightning leaves a blue streak in the sky, so **to talk a blue streak** means to talk as fast as lightning.

## With No Loss of Time

- before you can say Jack Robinson
- in two shakes of a lamb's tail
- time is of the essence
- to make hay while the sun shines

2   In a story from the *Canterbury Tales* a blacksmith is encouraged **to strike while the iron is hot**. After heating iron to a glow over a fire, if the blacksmith delayed shaping the metal with his hammer, the metal would cool. Then he would have to start the process of "heat and hammer" all over. Time would be lost, and the blacksmith would make less money that day.

## With Hardly Any Time Left

- by the skin of one's teeth
- in the nick of time
- at the eleventh hour
- nip and tuck
- touch and go

3   **Just under the wire** is a saying that comes from horse racing. Do you remember that *scratch* is the line at the beginning of a race? Well, the wire is the imaginary line at the end of a horse race. Sometimes horses are so close at the end of the last lap that the nose of the first horse to come "under the wire" wins. Nowadays we use the term "photo finish." Either saying means *barely made it in time*.

## Sleepy Time

- take forty winks
- asleep at the switch
- 'till the cows come home

4   Picture a tall candle with an amber flame burning the wick. Before electricity was common in homes, people used candles to light the night. Most candles were handmade and quite expensive. After sunset families generally ate their dinner by the glow from the fireplace, then went to bed. Candles were used only for important reasons such as nighttime reading.

5   When students **burn the candle at both ends** this means that they study very late into the evening and then get up before the sun rises to study again.

## Comprehension

An **opinion** is a statement that may or may not be true. It is what a person believes and is not necessarily a fact. Sentences with words such as *always, never, should, like, everyone,* or *all* may sound like facts, but they can also state opinions. A **fact** is something that can be proven to be true. Write **O** before the sentences that are opinions. Write **F** before the sentences that are facts.

1. ____ *The Canterbury Tales* was written in the fourteenth century.

2. ____ Sunsets are beautiful.

3. ____ *Scratch* is an imaginary line at the beginning of a race.

4. ____ Everyone likes to go to horse races.

5. ____ It's always good to take forty winks before dinner.

6. ____ Many European folk sayings have been Americanized.

## Vocabulary Development

Find the word in the paragraph in parentheses that best fits each definition given below.

1. involving much money; costly (4)

____

2. in the present time or age (3) _____

3. people who leave their native country and move to another (1) _____

4. one who shoes horses (2) _____

5. nighttime (5) _____

6. a picture taken with a camera (3)

____

## Reading Skills

To make a singular noun possessive add **'s**. *Possessive* means a person, place, or thing owns or has something. Fill in each blank with the **possessive** form of the noun in parentheses.

1. The _____ hammer weighed six pounds. (blacksmith)

2. Two days before the _____ test he ran out of candles. (student)

3. The_____ iron shoes were worn through. (horse)

4. A century ago an _____ tale might have included Ellis Island. (immigrant)

Find **compound words** in the paragraphs below:

5. (2) _____
6. (3) _____
7. (4) _____
8. (4) _____
9. (4) _____
10. (4) _____

## Study Skills

Words listed in alphabetical order in a dictionary are called **entry words**. To easily find an entry word you need to look at the **guide words** at the top of each page. Circle the correct set of guide words for each entry word.

1. **switch**
   swat-swizzle        swallow-swim

2. **delay**
   decide-degree       deduce-demand

3. **wink**
   widow-wind          wing-winter

4. **candle**
   canal-cannon        cane-cannot

5. **iron**
   iris-Iroquois       Iran-irksome

# From **"The Village Blacksmith"**

Can you think of jobs people don't do anymore?

Henry Wadsworth Longfellow was a nineteenth-century American poet. He was born
nearly a hundred years before cars were
invented. Back then most villages and towns
had a blacksmith who was kept busy shoeing
horses. Longfellow wrote this poem about an
honest blacksmith and how "time passes by."

1  Under a spreading chestnut-tree
The village smithy stands;
The smith, a mighty man is he,
With large and sinewy hands;
And the muscles of his brawny arms
Are strong as iron bands.

2  His hair is crisp, and black, and long,
His face is like the tan;
His brow is wet with honest sweat,
He earns whate'er he can,
And looks the whole world in the face,
For he owes not any man.

3  Week in, week out, from morn till night,
You can hear his bellows blow;
You can hear him swing his heavy sledge,
With measured beat and slow,
Like a sexton ringing the village bell,
When the evening sun is low.

4  And children coming home from school
Look in at the open door;
They love to see the flaming forge,
And hear the bellows roar,
And catch the burning sparks that fly
Like chaff from a threshing-floor.

5  He goes on Sunday to the church,
And sits among his boys;
He hears the parson pray and preach,
He hears his daughter's voice,
Singing in the village choir,
And it makes his heart rejoice.

6  It sounds to him like her mother's voice,
Singing in Paradise!
He needs must think of her once more,
How in the grave she lies;
And with his hard, rough hand he wipes
A tear out of his eyes.

7  Toiling,—rejoicing,—sorrowing
Onward through life he goes;
Each morning sees some task begin,
Each evening sees it close;
Something attempted, something done,
Has earned a night's repose.

www.summerbridgeactivities.com   Reading Connection—Grade 4—RBP0199

## Comprehension

1. **Character traits** are words that describe a person or animal in a story. Traits can describe how something looks, acts, feels, etc. Write whom these words describe in "The Village Blacksmith."

   honest          sad          fatherly

   _____

2. Write the sentence in the poem that tells you the blacksmith's wife is dead.

   _____

   _____

3. Check the sentence that **best** states the main idea of the poem.
   ____ All blacksmiths go to church.
   ____ A blacksmith has a hard life.
   ____ A blacksmith's life is like the ticking of a clock.

Circle the word that **best** completes each sentence.

4. The blacksmith _____ when he thought about his wife.
   laughed          cried          bellowed

5. The blacksmith's daughter liked to _____.
   dance          pray          sing

6. The village bell rang in the _____.
   evening          afternoon          morning

## Vocabulary Development

Find the word in the paragraph in parentheses that best fits each definition given below.

1. a janitor of a church (3) _____
2. beating stalks of ripened grain (4)

   _____

3. the tufts of grain (4) _____
4. resting; sleeping (7) _____
5. a preacher; minister (5) _____
6. cord-like (1) _____

## Reading Skills

A **prefix** is added to the beginning of a word to change its meaning. The prefix **pre-** means "before." For example, *prefix* means to "fix before." Add **pre-** to each word below. Then write the meaning of the word.

1. _____ wash _____
2. _____ school _____
3. _____ game _____
4. _____ view _____
5. _____ war _____
6. _____ date _____

Complete each sentence below with one of the words from above.

7. Janie was too young for kindergarten, so she went to _____.

8. Sam and his dad saw the _____ show at the basketball arena.

## Study Skills

Study the map of a historical nineteenth-century village; then answer the questions.

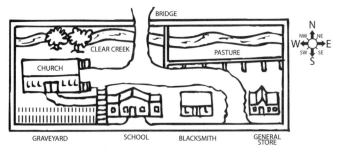

1. Which building is on the east side of the village? _____

2. Does the stream run north or south of the village? _____

3. If the blacksmith wanted to visit his wife's grave would he go north across the bridge or west toward the church? _____

4. When the parson visits the school does he leave the church and go southeast or northwest? _____

# Galileo
Don't drop meatballs off your roof!

---

## 1564
Galileo is born in Pisa, Italy.

Shakespeare is born in England.

1    "Hurry, Vincenzio, or we'll miss the demonstration at the leaning tower," said Maffeo.

2    In Pisa, Italy, there is an eight-story, round tower. However, instead of standing straight like most towers do, this one leans steeply to one side. The boys were racing along the cobblestone streets to see Galileo (Ga-lee-lay-oh) drop meatballs of different weights into a huge bowl of spaghetti. Galileo thought that heavy meatballs would not fall faster than light meatballs. The tower was the perfect place to drop meatballs to see if they landed at the same time.

3    At age 20, Galileo amazed mathematicians in Europe when he discovered a simple law of nature. One day at church he noticed a lantern swaying back and forth. Placing his finger on his wrist, he timed the swing with the beat of his heart. He discovered that each swing, whether long or short, took an equal amount of time. This simple fact was called the Law of the Pendulum. It led to the invention of the pendulum clock 73 years later.

4    Galileo was well-known in Pisa, where he was a student at the university. He was unpopular with the Catholic Church because he questioned its teaching that the planets and the sun rotated around Earth.

5    Galileo was trying to prove that Aristotle (Air-is-tot-el), a great Greek thinker, was incorrect. Aristotle had taught that heavy objects fall to earth faster than lighter objects. Galileo had planned a public experiment to prove that objects would fall at the same speed. His sister had stayed up all night making meatballs.

6    Panting for breath, Maffeo and Vincenzio entered the crowded plaza where the tower stood. They watched as Galileo dropped two huge meatballs of different weights at the same time. Along with the rest of the crowd, the boys gasped when the balls hit the pasta at the same time. Spaghetti sauce was everywhere!

7    Galileo was one of the most brilliant men to ever live. But the next day he was kicked out of the university for proving that Aristotle was wrong. He never ate meatballs again.

---

## 1641
Galileo dies at age 77.

Isaac Newton is born in England.

---

Editors note: Galileo actually used metal balls, not meatballs—but meatballs would work!

© RBP Books          www.summerbridgeactivities.com          Reading Connection—Grade 4—RBP0199

## Comprehension

1. An **opinion** is a statement that someone believes to be true but might not actually be true. What is the opinion in paragraph 7?_____
_____
_____

2. In the 1500s were young people encouraged to question what they were taught? Use a sentence from "Galileo" to support your answer._____
_____
_____

3. Why did Galileo put his finger on his wrist to feel his heartbeat? _____
_____
_____

4. Why did the author write this story?
____ to tell how you can question what you are taught
____ to tell about part of Galileo's life
____ to encourage you to drop objects off your roof

## Vocabulary Development

Write the letter of the correct definition in front of the word that matches.

1. ____ steeply
2. ____ experiment
3. ____ university
4. ____ cobblestone
5. ____ mathematician

A. a person who studies numbers
B. rock paving
C. school after high school
D. a test; experiment
E. sharply; dizzying

A **proper noun** names a specific person, place, or thing. Write two proper nouns from paragraph 2.

6. _____

7. _____

## Reading Skills

A **prefix** is added in front of a word to change its meaning. The prefixes **un-** and **in-** mean "not" or "without." For example, *unpleasant* means "not pleasant." Write the meaning of the following words.

1. incorrect _____
2. unpopular _____
3. unhappy _____
4. unwanted _____
5. unload _____

Write a **compound word** using two words from each sentence.

6. Galileo hit his finger when he was hammering a nail. _____

7. He timed the swing with the beat of his heart. _____

8. Italians add meat rolled into balls to pasta. _____

## Study Skills

Galileo was one of the first people to watch the skies through a telescope. For the next twelve days look for the moon, even during the day. Carefully date and color in the moons below.

1.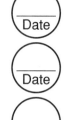

2. As the moon gets larger (waxing), does it add light on your right or your left?_____

3. As the moon gets smaller (waning), does the moon lose light on your right or your left?_____

# On the Move

Do you ever migrate?

1    *Migration* is when large groups of animals move from one place to another and back again. Birds, butterflies, elk, whales, salmon, and plankton all migrate. Scientists are still studying what makes so many animals do this. They know two things for sure: daylight and temperature changes have important effects on animal movement.

2    Humans used to migrate from cool northern mountains to warmer southerly plains as the seasons changed. But now we have well-built houses with furnaces to keep us warm and air conditioners to keep us cool. We can have a foot of snow covering our vegetable garden and still go to the store to buy fresh lettuce and tomatoes.

3    Until about one hundred years ago Native Americans followed the seasons. As daylight grew longer and snow began to melt, the Shoshone would pack up their homes and move north. Sometimes they went as far as Canada. Then, as the maple leaves turned crimson, the Shoshone would gather nuts and berries. The men would hunt migrating deer, elk, and rabbits with thick winter coats. The women would dry the meat and prepare the skins for clothing. When they were ready, some Shoshone tribes would trek south into warm desert lands.

4    In the western United States ranchers herd cattle and sheep onto the high mesas for summer grazing. Shepherds, with their colorful wagons, can occasionally be seen watching the flocks. In the fall ranchers drive the animals to the valley floors for overwintering.

5    One interesting migratory animal is plankton. Plankton are simple-celled creatures that are ruled by the sun. They are a major food source for other ocean animals. The enormous blue whale eats almost nothing but plankton. As daylight touches the surface of the ocean plankton sink deeper into the water, away from sunlight. Later in the day, as night approaches, the plankton slowly rise to the surface.

6    On March 19, or St. Joseph's Day, swallows arrive to rebuild their mud nests in the ruins of an old stone church. The church is in the little village of San Juan Capistrano along the coast of California. The town is overrun by visitors each March who come to see this "miracle of nature."

7    Scout swallows arrive a few days ahead of the main flock. They circle the roofless building and then fly off to lead the rest of the swallows home. On October 23, the Day of San Juan, the swallows take flight and head for a warmer climate.

8    Legend says that when the swallows first land in the spring the giant yellow flowers of the celandine plant burst open. Then, as the last swallow flies away in the autumn, the plants wither and fall to the ground.

© RBP Books          www.summerbridgeactivities.com          Reading Connection—Grade 4—RBP0199

Name _____          Date _____

## Comprehension

Circle the best answer for each question.

1. What is the name of the flower that bursts open when the swallows arrive?
   tomatoes     berries          celandine

2. Which animal did the Shoshone hunt?
   moose        elk              cougars

3. What is the main idea in this story?
   swallows     migration        plankton

4. What is a major cause for migration?
   the moon     daylight         ocean tides

5. Write a comparison between shepherds and the Shoshone. _____

   _____

   _____

6. What do you think the author means by "miracle of nature"?_____

   _____

   _____

## Vocabulary Development

**Synonyms** are words with similar meanings. Circle each pair of synonyms.

1. cattle—steer        2. arrive—leave

3. garden—field        4. store—shop

Match the number in front of each word with the correct definition.

5. wither      _____ a long hike or journey

6. trek        _____ bright red

7. mesa        _____ to shrink or wilt

8. crimson     _____ wide

9. overwinter  _____ a flat-topped hill

10. broad      _____ to keep something alive
                     from fall to spring

## Reading Skills

Write the **base word** for each word below.

1. visitors_____

2. migratory_____

3. northern_____

4. southerly_____

5. The suffix -**less** means "without." Find the word in paragraph 7 that has the suffix -**less**. Write the word and its meaning.

   word: _____

   meaning: _____

6. The prefix **re-** means "to do again." Find the word in paragraph 6 that has the prefix **re-**. Write the word and its meaning.

   word: _____

   meaning: _____

## Study Skills

Study the map above and answer the questions.

1. Is San Juan Capistrano north or south of San Francisco? _____

2. What state is north of California?

   _____

3. Which direction would you go to reach Los Angeles from the Old Stone Church?

   _____

4. From your state which direction would you go if you wanted to see the swallows migrate?_____

50

**Reading Connection—Grade 4—RBP0199**          www.summerbridgeactivities.com          ©RBP Books

# Fables about Time

Do you know any fables?

1   In about 620 B.C. a slave was born in ancient Greece. This slave, **Aesop**, eventually was granted his freedom in honor of his great wisdom. After Aesop died in the year 565 B.C. about 200 of his fables were compiled into a set called *Assemblies of Aesopic Tales*. A **fable** is a brief tale that uses animals and humans to teach a moral.

## The Girl and the Almonds

2   A girl, hungry after a day of play, spied a jar of honeyed almonds sitting on the kitchen table. "Mom, may I please have some nuts?" she asked, her ravenous tummy growling.

3   "It's almost time for dinner," said her mother. "Only take a handful."

4   The greedy little girl reached into the jar, grabbing as many nuts as her fingers could hold. But when she tried to pull out her bulging hand, it got stuck in the narrow neck of the jar. Twisting and turning, she tugged until her arm grew sore and tears of disappointment flowed down her cheeks.

5   Amazed at her daughter's stubbornness, her mother said, "Let go of half the almonds, or you will end up with none at all."

**Moral: A little at a time is better than none at all.**

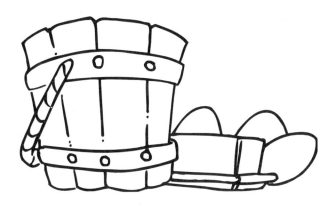

## The Milkmaid and Her Pail

6   A young milkmaid was walking down a dusty path with a pail of fresh, warm cow's milk poised upon her head. As she neared her small thatched hut, daydreams filled her mind.

7   "The milk was so creamy this morning," she thought. "I'll churn the cream into golden butter which I will sell at the village market tomorrow. With the money I make from the butter I will buy a dozen eggs, and from the dozen eggs will hatch a dozen chickens. The dozen chickens will each lay a dozen eggs, and then I will have chickens, eggs, and butter to sell at the Autumn Fair.

8   "With the money I make at the fair I will buy a silver gown embroidered with pearls. This winter I will wear it to the Sheriff's Ball. When his son sees me, he'll seek me to dance. But will I? Oh, never! As he begs to take my hand I'll sweetly smile and shake my head from side to side—like this!"

9   In that moment, the milkmaid's dreams turned back to reality. The wooden pail lay broken on the ground, and so in the end, she had nothing, not even the milk she had started with.

**Moral: Pay attention to the present so the future might be what you dream.**

## Comprehension

1. Check the sentence that best tells the main idea of "The Girl and the Almonds."
   ____ Listen to what your mother says.
   ____ Store nuts in a wide-mouthed jar.
   ____ Don't be greedy.

2. Check the sentence that best tells the main idea of "The Milkmaid and Her Pail."
   ____ Check the sidewalk for rocks.
   ____ Pay attention to what you are doing.
   ____ Don't dream dreams.

Check the **cause** (what makes something happen) for the **effect** (what happened).

3. The milkmaid drops the pail.
   ____ She trips on the path.
   ____ She shakes her head.
   ____ She spills the milk.

4. The girl's hand is stuck in the jar.
   ____ The neck of the jar is too wide.
   ____ There are too many nuts in the jar.
   ____ There are too many nuts in her hand.

5. Does the milkmaid like the sheriff's son? Write a sentence that answers yes or no.
   _____
   _____

## Vocabulary Development

A **homophone** is a word that sounds exactly the same as another word but has a different spelling. Circle the correct homophone to complete each sentence.

1. After Aesop _____ his fables became famous throughout the world.
   died              dyed

2. It is difficult to balance a wooden _____ on one's head.
   pale              pail

3. When you daydream, your _____ wanders away from present time.
   mined             mind

## Reading Skills

The following words can be found in "The Girl and the Almonds" and "The Milkmaid and Her Pail." Write the **base word** for each word.

1. creamy            _____
2. grabbing          _____
3. reality           _____
4. stubbornness      _____
5. bulging           _____
6. honeyed           _____
7. dusty             _____
8. spied             _____
9. sweetly           _____
10. broken           _____

## Study Skills

Use the dictionary entries below to answer the questions.

**Ravenous** *adj.* (ra-vɛn-ɛs) extremely hungry for food.

1. What part of speech is the word *ravenous*?
   _____

2. Write a sentence using *ravenous*.
   _____
   _____

3. How many syllables does *ravenous* have?
   _____

**Poise** *v.* (poiz) 1. to hold in balance. 2. to hold in readiness for action.

4. How many syllables are there in *poise*?
   _____

5. Write the first definition in the entry.
   _____

6. What part of speech is the word *poise*?
   _____

**Reading Connection—Grade 4—RBP0199**          www.summerbridgeactivities.com          © RBP Books

# More Fables about Time

What can you learn from a thirsty bird?

Aesop was a wise man who understood how important time is in everyday life. Here are two more fables about time.

## The Boy Who Went Swimming

1  During the dog days of August a boy was walking alone along the banks of a deep river. Despite all the warnings from his parents to never swim in the river, he could not resist the temptation of the cool water. As soon as he was a few feet from the sandy shore, he realized the current was swifter than he had imagined.

2  Enormous rocks appeared ahead as the boy struggled to grab a branch of one of the cotton-woods that dotted the bank. Kicking and splashing, he spotted an old woman washing her clothes on a large rock. "Help!" he shouted.

3  "You are crazy to go swimming in this river," said the woman as she waggled a finger at him. "Wait till I tell your parents how you disobeyed them. Boy, you're in big trouble. What would have happened to you if I hadn't been here doing my laundry? Let me tell you, when I was a young girl—"

4  "Madame, please!" cried the boy. "Save my life now and lecture me all you want later!"

**Moral: There is a time and place for every-thing.**

## The Raven and the Pitcher

5  For months and months rain had failed to fall in the high desert country. The cacti's fleshy leaves, always a source of water for thirsty animals, had dried and withered into flat, leathery discs. Creeks and pools shaded by the red rock canyons had turned to clay.

6  A raven, gray with dust, circled high above in the parched sky. Weak from thirst, he knew that death would come by sunset if he could not find water. Spotting something shining in a deserted campsite below, the raven swooped down. It was a glass pitcher half-filled with liquid! But when the raven put his beak into the pitcher he couldn't reach the water.

7  Now desperate, he perched beside the container and thought and thought until he had an idea. Grabbing a small pebble from the ground, he dropped it into the pitcher. Then he dropped another pebble into the pitcher. Then he dropped another pebble into the pitcher. Then he dropped another pebble into the pitcher. Pebble by pebble he watched as the water rose closer to the top until, at last, he was able to drink his fill and save his life.

**Moral: Some of the hardest problems are solved a little at a time.**

www.summerbridgeactivities.com    Reading Connection—Grade 4—RBP0199

## Comprehension

To **infer** or **make an inference** is to *arrive at an answer using information that you know from past experiences*. When you make an inference about something you have read, the answer **will not** be directly in the story.

1. In "The Boy Who Went Swimming" was it hot or cold outside? How do you know?

   _____

   _____

2. In "The Raven and The Pitcher" why was the raven desperate? How do you know?

   _____

   _____

Circle the word that **best** completes the sentence.

3. The man was hungry and _____ to find some food.

   sad        desperate        soon

4. The athlete threw a ____ forty yards.

   referee      bat      disc

## Vocabulary Development

Find the word in the paragraph in parentheses that best fits each definition given below.

1. this tries to get a person do something unwise or evil (1)

   _____

2. plump; fat (5) _____

3. a tree native to America (2) _____

   _____

4. water that is moving (1)

   _____

5. became limp when not watered (5)

   _____

## Reading Skills

When a noun ends in **-us**, to make the word plural you drop the **-us** and add **i**. For example, a *cactus* becomes *cacti*.

Write the plural form for the following nouns.

1. octopus _____
2. bronchus _____
3. fungus _____
4. nimbus _____
5. radius _____

A **suffix** is added to the end of a base word to change its meaning. The suffix **-est** means "the most." For example *hardest* means "the most hard." Add **-est** to each word below. Then write its meaning.

6. sweet _____ means _____
7. soft _____ means _____
8. dark _____ means _____
9. full _____ means _____
10. light _____ means _____

## Study Skills

A library's computer is a **reference system**, like dictionaries and encyclopedias. Books in the library can be found many different ways. One way is by **main subject**. If you wanted to find more books about Aesop, what other subjects could you look up besides Aesop?

1. _____

2. _____

3. Number the words below in alphabetical order.

   ____ perch      ____ pitcher

   ____ river       ____ realize

   ____ swift       ____ swim

   ____ raven      ____ pebble

   ____ parch      ____ pool

Reading Connection—Grade 4—RBP0199      www.summerbridgeactivities.com      ©RBP Books

# The Flight of the Monarch

Do you know where butterflies spend the winter?

1   She's only four inches wide and thin as tissue paper. You would need five of her to equal the weight of one penny, and in sunlight she's transparent. She looks delicate, but she not! She's a tough little migratory machine. Named after a king, she's an autumn monarch butterfly.

2   Unable to survive the freezing winters in the northern states, she begins her flight to the high mountains of Mexico as soon as her wings have dried in the warm August sun. Flying at speeds of up to 20 miles per hour, she can cover almost 80 miles a day. She will rest at night, then feed on nectar and water before continuing her journey.

3   After soaring southward for two months, she will come to her winter home on a mountain called Cerro Pelon. Tens of millions of monarchs will take the same journey. Once they arrive, they rest and huddle together for warmth and protection for about four months.

4   As the days lengthen and the air heats up, the monarchs will mate. Then the females will begin their flight north. A female will lay as many as 500 eggs on milkweed plants all across the United States. After traveling up to 4,000 miles, the butterfly's life will end in early spring. Then the cycle begins again.

5   Caterpillars hatch from the butterfly eggs and eat the milkweed leaves. Milkweed contains a sticky white fluid that contains a poison. When a caterpillar eats the milkweed leaves, the poison enters into its body. Small amounts of this substance are passed to the adult butterfly. The bright orange-red color on the monarch's wings is a warning to predators to stay away.

Predators of the monarch include the black-eared mouse, blue jays, black-beaked grosbeak, and orioles.

6   If you want monarch butterflies to spend time in your garden, you should grow milkweed. Milkweed leaves are all the monarch caterpillar eats. Most gardeners think milkweed is a bothersome plant. But just one milkweed plant hidden away in a corner is all the female monarch needs. The plant's scent will lead the butterfly to the perfect spot, where she will lay a single jewel-like egg. A butterfly's egg is about the size of a pinhead.

7   The caterpillar comes equipped with powerful jaws it uses to chomp through the furry milkweed leaves. The butterfly doesn't have jaws. It sips nectar from flowers using a straw-like mouth called a *proboscis*.

## Mary, Mary, How Does Your Garden Grow?

Plant plenty of the flowers listed below to attract monarchs to your garden:

- marigold
- aster
- cornflower
- phlox
- butterfly weed (milkweed)
- cosmos
- zinnia
- sunflower
- honeysuckle

© RBP Books          www.summerbridgeactivities.com          Reading Connection—Grade 4—RBP0199

## Comprehension

1. Fill in the blanks to complete the life cycle of the autumn monarch butterfly.

   As soon as her _____ are dry an autumn monarch begins to _____ south. Flying about _____ each day, she will reach a mountain called _____ in two months. During the _____ season she will _____. Sometime in late February or early _____ she will migrate _____ to the United States. After laying about 500 _____ she will then _____.

2. How do you think *milkweed* got its name?
   _____
   _____

3. If gardeners killed all the milkweed, what would happen to the monarch butterfly and why? _____
   _____
   _____

## Vocabulary Development

Find the word in the paragraph shown in parentheses that best fits the description.

1. (6) to be annoying _____

2. (3) rising high in the air _____

3. (5) material from which something is made _____

4. (7) a sugary liquid found in flowers
   _____

5. (7) to have whatever is needed for a task
   _____

6. (1) easily seen through _____

7. (2) crowd together _____

## Reading Skills

Write the two words that make up the **compound words** found in the paragraph shown in the parentheses.

1. (6) _____ and _____

2. (4) _____ and _____

3. (6) _____ and _____

4. (6) _____ and _____

5. Find the **context clue** in paragraph 7 that tells you the meaning of *proboscis*.
   _____

## Study Skills

Study the **table of contents** below; then answer the questions.

### The Autumn Butterfly

1. What chapter looks most interesting to you and why? _____
   _____
   _____

2. If you wanted to learn how to follow a butterfly, on which page would you start to read?
   _____

3. By looking at the table of contents you can tell that not everything is known about butterflies. Write the name of the chapter that gives this hint. _____
   _____

Would you like to travel through time?

# Book Review

### By Charles Sport
*The Zipper Press*

1    Last weekend, as rain dripped from the sky, I read *A Wrinkle in Time* by Madeleine L'Engle. I was transported from a windy autumn night on Earth to planets in galaxies far from ours. The main characters are Meg; her little brother, Charles Wallace; and Calvin, a high school basketball player. They team up with the strange trio of Mrs. Whatsit, Mrs. Who, and Mrs. Which to fight the Black Thing.

2    A cold shadow lurks as the Black Thing plunges planet after planet into darkness, turning the inhabitants into human robots. Meg's father, who has been studying time travel with the U.S. government, is captured by this thing. He is being held on the planet Camazotz. Nearly a year later, his life depends on Meg, a friendless teenager who struggles with schoolwork. Charles Wallace, a six-year-old genius, complicates the rescue when he is taken hostage, too.

3    The three ladies, some of the most delightful characters ever, gave up their lives as stars to battle the Black Thing. Mrs. Whatsit, the youngest, is fond of dressing up in wacky earthling clothes. She says to the children, "I didn't mean to tell you. But, oh my dears, I did so love being a star."

4    Mrs. Whatsit, Mrs. Who, and Mrs. Which whisk the children around space by wrinkling time. Traveling through time, or *tessering*, is easy according to Mrs. Whatsit. It seems easy, until Mrs. Which mistakenly lands everyone on a planet that is only two dimensional. The children flatten out like sheets of paper, unable to think or breathe. They are saved moments later by another wrinkle.

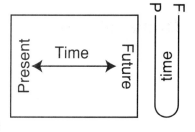

5    To understand wrinkling time, take a piece of paper and write **present** on the left side and **future** on the right side. The space between is *time*. Now, fold or wrinkle the paper so the two words come together. The present touches the future with no time between. This is the fifth dimension, or as Mrs. Whatsit calls it, a *tesseract*. This is a wrinkle in time.

6    Madeleine L'Engle, who won the Newberry Award for this book, has studied Albert Einstein's Theory of Relativity. In *A Wrinkle in Time*, she gives kids a peek at time travel without the mind-boggling confusion of advanced math. At one point, Mrs. Whatsit assures Meg that they've taken a "nice tidy wrinkle and they'll be back to Earth five minutes before they left." Unless, of course, "something goes terribly wrong; then it won't matter if they ever get back at all."

7    Mr. Sport is a free-lance writer for Zipper Press and submitted this review from his home in Park City, Utah.

## Comprehension

Check the space that tells the main idea in the given paragraph.

1. Paragraph 3:
   ____ Mrs. Whatsit loved wacky clothes.
   ____ Mrs. Whatsit is a lovable character.
   ____ Mrs. Whatsit once was a star.

2. Paragraph 5:
   ____ The fifth dimension is when there is no time between the present and future.
   ____ Mrs. Whatsit calls the fifth dimension a tesseract.
   ____ You need to fold a piece of paper.

3. Paragraph 1:
   ____ Charles Sport loved reading *A Wrinkle in Time*.
   ____ Last weekend it rained the whole time.
   ____ A group of people are fighting the Black Thing.

4. Write one way Charles Wallace and Meg are different. Use a complete sentence.

   _____
   _____

## Vocabulary Development

A **homophone** is a word that sounds the same as another word but has a different meaning and spelling. Write the correct homophone (shown in parentheses) in the blank.

1. Meg pulled hard on the horse's _____. (rain, rein)

2. The girls _____ their basketball game. (one, won)

3. The math test will last one _____. (hour, our)

4. Circle the best meaning for *inhabitants* in paragraph 2:
   people          bad habits          planets

## Reading Skills

When a noun is plural and it owns or has something it becomes a **plural possessive noun**. If the plural form of the noun ends in **s**, simply add an apostrophe to the end of the noun. For example, for "dogs have bones," you can write "**dogs'** bones."

Write the possessive plural for the following words.

1. planet      _____
2. traveler    _____
3. hostage     _____
4. book        _____
5. brother     _____

The suffix **-ness** when added to the end of a noun gives the noun a state of being. For example, the state of being kind is *kindness*. Write the meaning of these words.

1. darkness    _____
2. fondness    _____
3. easiness    _____

## Study Skills

An **encyclopedia** is a set of reference books that organizes subjects alphabetically. Information about people is found by looking up a last name first. Write which volume you would look at to research information for each topic.

| Vol 1 | Vol 2 | Vol 3 | Vol 4 | Vol 5 | Vol 6 |
|-------|-------|-------|-------|-------|-------|
| A-D   | E-G   | H-L   | M-P   | R-T   | U-Z   |

1. ___ basketball      2. ___ Madeleine L'Engle

3. ___ stars           4. ___ witches

# The Day of the Bear

What do you want to be when you grow up?

1    Rose had risen early. A thunderbolt from an early morning storm had pulled her rudely back from dreamland, and once awake she felt an urge to be outside. Morning was certainly her favorite time of day. Here at the cabin, on a high meadow overlooking the Merced River, it was quiet until about noon. That's when her brothers and sisters, all teenagers, would finally crawl out of the numerous bunk beds that filled the sleeping loft. Rose was the baby of the family, and in her opinion that was a dreadful thing to be.

2    She eased out the back door and slid silently into the surrounding woods. Walking on the tips of her toes, Rose made as little noise as possible. Out of the corner of her eye she saw a bush move ever so slightly and heard the rustle of fallen needles on the mossy forest floor. Creeping closer, she saw a deer with a white-spotted fawn munching the delicate new leaves of a winterberry shrub. SNAP! As Rose's foot stepped on a dry twig, the mother raised her tail in a white flash before running away.

3    "Drats," said Rose. "At this rate I'm never going to get close to her baby." Since coming to the summer lodge a week ago, Rose had been playing hide-and-seek with the doe and her newborn. "He'll lose all his spots before I have time to count them!" she thought.

4    More than anything else in the world Rose wanted to be a forest ranger. Sure, she loved the wildflowers and the sweet piney scent that the trees gave off after a storm. Sure, she could sit still for hours on a tree stump watching a chipmunk gather acorns for its winter stash. But mostly, she wanted to be a ranger because she hated CLOCKS!

5    Her parents were both engineers who constantly talked about difficult mathematical puzzles involving time and space. To make matters worse, all of her seven brothers and sisters were math whizzes, winning dozens of state and national awards. She, on the other hand, was nine and still hadn't memorized her addition tables, much less her times tables. Tired from useless hours of flashing number cards in front of her, her mom was constantly asking, "What are we going to do with you, Rose?"

6    However, her main problem wasn't so much math facts as it was her watch. With eight children in the house, her parents coped by running everything "by the clock." Each day as her father scooted the family into their hotel-size van, he would say, "Ship-shape, on time." Rose had absolutely no idea what he was talking about.

7    As soon as each child learned to talk, Rose's parents attached a little Mickey Mouse watch on their left wrist. And, of course, they just expected Rose to learn how to tell time. The other seven had learned to tell time down to the millisecond by the time they were three, so why not Rose?

*(to be continued)*

www.summerbridgeactivities.com                    Reading Connection—Grade 4—RBP0199

## Comprehension

Write an answer for each question below.

1. Why did Rose get up so early?

   _____

   _____

2. What do you think "running everything by the clock" means?_____

   _____

   _____

3. Is a hotel-size van a minivan or an extra large van? Explain your answer. _____

   _____

   _____

4. Write a comparison between Rose and one of her older brothers. Use the word *while* in your sentence. _____

   _____

   _____

## Vocabulary Development

Check the correct meaning of the underlined word.

1. Rose thought it was the most <u>dreadful</u> thing to be.
   ____ marvelous         ____ terrible
   ____ wonderful         ____ sad

2. She felt the <u>urge</u> to be outside.
   ____ sun               ____ deer
   ____ desire            ____ thunder

3. Rose's brothers and sisters were math <u>whizzes</u>.
   ____ drones            ____ teachers
   ____ nerds             ____ experts

4. The chipmunk <u>stashed</u> its acorns.
   ____ hid               ____ spent
   ____ used              ____ ate

## Reading Skills

Write the possessive form for the words below.

1. brothers        _____

2. Rose            _____

3. lodge           _____

4. sisters         _____

5. engineers       _____

6. children        _____

7. deer            _____

8. baby            _____

9. Write the two words that make the compound word in paragraph 2: _____ and _____. Compound words are sometimes easier to understand when you break them down into smaller words.

   What do you think a winterberry looks like? _____

   _____

## Study Skills

Check the word that you would find on the same page as the guide words below.

1. fate-feat
   ____ fat        ____ fawn        ____ feather

2. moose-most
   ____ moon       ____ mother      ____ moss

3. scary-scholar
   ____ scent      ____ scale       ____ school

4. delay-delivery
   ____ delta      ____ delicate    ____ deity

What is something you do very well?

8    Rose's spring parent-teacher conference had gone badly. "What do you mean *she can't tell time*?" said her father. "Everyone knows how to tell time."

9    "Not Rose," said Miss Mays.

10    "There are clocks everywhere in our house," said her father. Holding up his hand he began to count off. "There's a clock in the kitchen and two in each bathroom. The laundry room has a plastic one, just in case a water hose breaks. Then there's the three-foot-wide clock on the garage wall so everyone can see it, coming and going. And look," he said as he grabbed Rose's arm. "She's had this watch on since she was eighteen months old ..."

11    "She can't tell time," insisted her teacher.

12    Dinner that night had started out as a quiet affair. Rose had felt like an alien eating lasagna and bread with a bunch of earthlings. The whole family slowly chewed their food and stared at her, stunned that numbers could be a mystery to anyone related to them.

13    Suddenly, words began to fall out of their mouths in a jumble, "No wonder she's always late ... she misses her laundry time and has to wear stinky clothes to school ... at night she brushes her teeth for twenty minutes and reads for two ... yesterday she microwaved the pop-corn for thirty minutes instead of three. Nothing was left except a smoking pile of ashes ..." and on and on.

14    Rose stood up from the table, undid the strap on Mickey, and dropped it, *splat!* Tomato sauce flew onto the tablecloth, and little red dots appeared on eyeglasses around the table. "I might not know much about clock time. But I do know a daddy longlegs spun a web full of eggs under this table, and they're about to hatch." Rose turned to run from the room,

as chairs were quickly pushed away from the dinner table, saying under her breath, "There is your kind of time and then there is my kind of time."

15    Since that night two months ago Rose's life had gotten easier. The flashcards grew dusty on a bookshelf. Her watch, minus the tomato sauce, was stored away in her father's desk. Beth, her oldest sister, bought Rose an alarm that ticked off the two minutes it took to brush her teeth, the twenty minutes she was to read each night, the nine hours needed for sleep. Someone always came and got her when it was her time for laundry, and no one let her any-where near the microwave.

16    The biggest change came a few weeks later when her brothers and sisters went out of state for Math Olympics, a national competition. That was when her parents decided to take Rose to the cabin. Just the three of them, no one else!

*(to be continued)*

## Comprehension

1. Circle the number that would best describe "a few."

   one            four            seven

2. Why was Rose's family so quiet at the table? _____
   _____
   _____

3. What were the red spots that appeared on the eyeglasses? _____

4. Why did the flashcards get dusty?
   _____
   _____

5. Write two sentences about how you think this story will end. _____
   _____
   _____
   _____

## Vocabulary Development

1. An **idiom** is a word or group of words that have a special meaning. Would your voice be loud or quiet if you said something "under your breath"? _____

Circle the word that does not belong.

2. washing       drying       singing    laundry

3. conference    parting      meeting    gathering

4. orderly       jumble       mess       confusion

5. competition   leave        meet       match

6. noodles       tomatoes     lasagna    apples

7. event         affair       going      activity

## Reading Skills

A **context clue** is a word or group of words that help you understand the meaning of another word. Write the context clue found in the paragraph in the parentheses for each word below.

1. alien (12) _____
   _____

2. laundry (10) _____
   _____

3. daddy longlegs (14) _____
   _____

4. What state do you live in? _____

5. Write the name of a state that is not your state. _____

6. Write the meaning of "out of state."
   _____

## Study Skills

Answer the questions below.

| Moss Landing School Conferences March 24, 2003 Miss Mays' Class | | | |
|---|---|---|---|
| Junie | 5:00 P.M. | Mary | 6:20 P.M. |
| Barb | 5:20 P.M. | Zita | 6:40 P.M. |
| Bill | 5:40 P.M. | Rose | 7:00 P.M. |
| Joey | 6:00 P.M. | Jack | 7:20 P.M. |

Knock softly on door if your time is past by five minutes.        *Note: No school tomorrow*

1. What school is having parent-teacher conferences? _____

2. What time is Junie's meeting with Miss Mays? _____

3. What should Rose's parents do if it is 7:05 P.M. and they still haven't met with Miss Mays? _____

4. What is happening on March 25 at Moss Landing School? _____

Reading Connection—Grade 4—RBP0199                 www.summerbridgeactivities.com        © RBP Books

Has there ever been a time you just knew it was going to rain?

18   A soft rain drizzled down through the pines as Rose led the way over the path. An hour ago she had been bouncing on her parents' feather bed trying to get them up and going. No one in her family was an early riser except for Rose. She woke with the sun rising and fell asleep with the sun setting. "I'm an early-gets-the-worm robin," thought Rose. "Mom and Dad are night owls."

19   "Rose, honey, where are we going? Is this really necessary? Don't you see how wet we're getting? Can't we go back to the cabin?"

20   Thoroughly enjoying herself, Rose said, "If you want to see anything you need to be a lot quieter, but to answer your questions … to the cave, yes, yes, and no." Just then she stopped, raising a finger to her lips. "Shhhh!"

21   Crossing the path several yards in front of them was a mother deer and her baby. Wobbling on four spindly legs, the fawn couldn't have been more than a day old. Hardly breathing, they watched as the deer nibbled at some early primroses that had managed to peek their heads up through the melting snow. After the deer had moved back into the forest, Rose's mother let out a long sigh and said, "That was a magnificent sight. I'm glad I got up early."

22   "Wait till you see what else you've been missing, sleepyheads," said Rose. The rain had stopped, and birds began to come out of their nests. Darting about overhead, mountain chickadees and blue jays searched for withered berries that had survived the winter. For several minutes they watched a gray squirrel attempt to rob a striped chipmunk's pile of nuts. Too weak and thin after living off his own fat during the long months of hibernation, the squirrel finally scampered off to eat some berries a jay had knocked to the ground.

23   Rose felt pride as her parents quizzed her about the wildlife that surrounded them. She knew each animal's name, what it ate, and where it slept. She was able to show her mom and dad flowers that were opening up their petals as the sun grew warmer and find birds high in the trees as they sang their morning songs. She didn't know math, and she certainly wasn't concerned about time. She knew, however, that she was special, and in the end that's all that really counts.

24   Scrambling up to the top of a bank of granite rock, Rose again said, "Shhhh!" Motioning her parents to sit, Rose handed them a granola bar and waited. Down below in the little glen an enormous brown creature appeared. Gasping with fright her mom said, "We need to get out of here!"

25   "It's fine, Mom," said Rose. "She's just coming out of hibernation. She's still too sleepy to run very fast. Look!"

26   Behind the mother bear, two baby cubs ambled out from their winter cave. Sniffing the air, they rolled in the rapidly disappearing snow. "Rose," said her dad. "How did you know they would come out today?"

27   "That's easy, Dad. It was time."

*The End*

   www.summerbridgeactivities.com    Reading Connection—Grade 4—RBP0199

## Comprehension

Answer each question in complete sentences.

1. In paragraph 18, Rose compares herself to a robin. What well-known saying about time does she use to describe the robin?
   _____
   _____

2. What animal does Rose compare her parents to and why? _____
   _____

3. Why was the gray squirrel weak and thin?
   _____
   _____

4. Rose's own clock seems to run on *nature's time*. Knowing that, why does it say in the beginning of the story, "she hates clocks"? Use a sentence from paragraph 18 to support your answer.
   _____
   _____

5. Rose's family had a hard time understanding that telling time and math were difficult for her. What made Rose realize that it was OK for her to be different? What feeling did she have when she made this discovery? _____
   _____

## Vocabulary Development

Write the word found in the paragraph shown in parentheses that best fits the definition.

1. walked slowly (26) _____

2. a valley (24) _____

3. a spring flower (21) _____

4. the act of sleeping through the winter (22)_____

## Reading Skills

Write the **base word** for the following words.

1. hibernation  _____

2. berries  _____

3. disappearing  _____

The suffix **dis-** means "not." Write the meaning of the words below.

4. disappearing  _____

5. disapprove  _____

6. dislike  _____

7. disloyal  _____

8. distasteful  _____

## Study Skills

Reading maps is helpful for finding your way around new places. Below is a map that Rose made while exploring the forest around her cabin. Study it and answer the questions below.

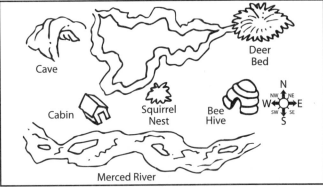

1. In what direction would you walk from the cabin to the deer's sleeping spot?
   _____

2. From the bears' cave, what direction would you go if you wanted to see the squirrel's nest?_____

3. What body of water is south of the cabin?
   _____

4. The honeybees' hive is _____ of the cabin.

# I'm Having the Time of My Life

How do you use your time?

A **timeline** is a graph that arranges events and the dates when those events happened. It begins with the earliest date and ends with the latest date.

Here is an example of a **time timeline**.

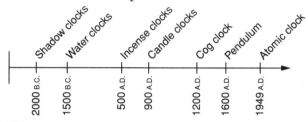

# Personal Timeline

You will need:
- pencils
- crayons
- a sheet of white paper; scratch paper
- a yardstick or big ruler
- pictures of yourself (optional)
- magazines (optional)

## Step 1

Make a list of all the important and interesting events that have happened in your life. Most people start with their birthday. Once you have some cool information written down, put all the dates in order.

## Step 2

Draw a line with your ruler all the way across the paper, about $\frac{1}{4}$ of the paper's width from the bottom. Now, draw a small vertical line at the far left-hand side of the longer line and an arrow at the far right-hand side. (**see timeline above**)

## Step 3

Add your dates, in order, below the timeline. Next, write the event that goes with each date above the timeline. Finally, draw pictures for each date or glue photos that match each time period.

**ART NOTE**

You can cut pictures from magazines and create collages instead of using photos or drawings.

When was the last time someone asked you *how you spent your time*?

Listen carefully, and you might hear a teacher ask a student who hasn't completed a project: "What have you been doing with your time?" Hopefully, that student isn't you because on many school report cards there is a section that tells if you *use time wisely*.

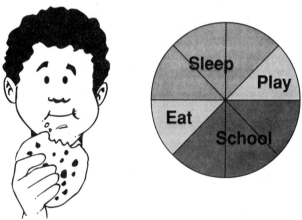

Here are two pie graphs for you to fill in, one for school days and the other for weekends. Each pie has been broken into eight three-hour sections. For a week, keep track of how you spend your time. Fill in the graphs by labeling each section with the activities *that take up your time* (see sample above). Lightly color sections with the same activity the same color.

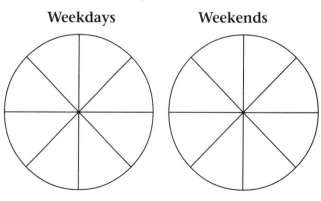

**Weekdays**      **Weekends**

   www.summerbridgeactivities.com    **Reading Connection—Grade 4—RBP0199**

## Comprehension

1. Number the directions in the order in which they are to be done.

   ____ Write the event that goes with the date above the timeline.

   ____ Make a list of important dates.

   ____ Draw a line all the way across the paper.

   ____ Draw pictures for each event.

2. What does the saying "How did you spend your time" mean?_____

   _____

3. After looking at your weekday pie chart, write what you spend the most time doing. Then write what you spend the least time doing. _____

   _____

4. When you made your personal timeline what did you learn about your life that you didn't know before?_____

   _____

## Vocabulary Development

A **homograph** is a word that is spelled the same as another word but has a different meaning. Choose the correct homograph for each set of meanings below.

| match | ruler | right |
|-------|-------|-------|

1. a. correct          b. good

   _____

2. a. a measuring device     b. a leader

   _____

3. a. a contest         b. look alike

   _____

4. What word in ART NOTE means "combination"?

   _____

## Reading Skills

Write the **base words** for the words below:

1. earliest          _____

2. latest           _____

3. longer           _____

4. activities         _____

5. Write the **compound word** in Step 1.

   _____

6. Write the **compound word** in Step 3.

   _____

## Study Skills

Reading directions is part of everyday life. The hardest part seems to be *reading all the directions* before starting a task. Read the directions below; then answer the questions.

**Fried Dandelion Heads**

| 1 | cup of dandelion heads |
| 4 | cups boiling water |
| 3 | tablespoons butter |
| $\frac{1}{4}$ | teaspoon salt |

Add the dandelion heads to the 4 cups boiling water. Immediately turn heat to low and simmer for ten minutes.

Meanwhile, slowly melt the butter in a frying pan. Drain the water off the dandelions and add them to the butter. Cook until tender, about five minutes. Add salt before serving.

1. What do you need to do first?

   _____

2. What goes in the frying pan last?

   _____

3. How much butter do you use?

   _____

# The National Air and Space Museum

Do you keep a diary?

---

National Air and Space Museum
Independence Ave. and 6th Street
Free Admission. Daily 10–5 P.M.

1 The Metro train whisked to a stop deep beneath the nation's capital. Roberto was so excited he had to remind himself to breathe. Two years ago he and his family had emigrated from Mexico to a small town in northern Utah. His father was a missile scientist who worked for NASA (National Air and Space Administration). He was developing new rockets for a space plane that would someday replace the shuttle.

2 As far back as Roberto could remember he had wanted to be an Air Force pilot. He had won a writing contest with an essay titled "Why Do I Want to Be an Air Force Pilot?" The prize was an "all-expenses-paid" trip to Washington, D.C. with his entire family. Today he was on his way to visit the National Air and Space Museum. Tomorrow he was going to meet the president of the United States!

3 "Hang on, Rosa," he said, grasping his sister's hand. The escalator rose steeply toward the morning light. The Air Force cadet who was escorting the family was explaining the subway. "Almost 30 years ago the first subway began running under the city," he said. "The subway averages over half a million riders each workday.

This has reduced pollution from car fumes. The exhaust was harming the marble and granite on the monuments."

4 Seven hours later the family returned to their hotel room across from the Capitol building. That evening they were going to see the city's monuments, which were lit up like shimmering jewels at night. The monuments honored past presidents and soldiers who had fought to keep our country free. But now, it was time to rest.

Open daily 10–5 P.M.
**FLIGHT LINE**
A cafeteria-style restaurant serving hot dogs, hamburgers, pizza, soda and ice cream.
Expect long lines at peak hours.

5 Roberto pulled out his diary and wrote:

6 *Today was one of the best days I've ever had. I saw the plane that Wilbur Wright flew over Kitty Hawk. I also saw* Glamorous Glennis, *the X-1 rocket plane that Chuck Yeager flew when he broke the sound barrier. The* Mercury *space capsule that Scott Carpenter used to orbit the earth was barely taller than my dad!*

7 *I don't think I could ever be that brave. When we were watching the movie* To Fly! *I really felt like I was a pilot. The screen is about five stories high, and sometimes I had to close my eyes as we zoomed around outer space.*

8 *And tomorrow I meet the president.*

www.summerbridgeactivities.com Reading Connection—Grade 4—RBP0199

## Comprehension

1. Did Roberto's family have to pay for their trip to Washington, D.C.? Use a sentence from the story to prove your answer.

   _____

   _____

2. Why did the family need to rest?

   _____

   _____

3. Why do you think the train in Washington, D.C. was built underground?

   _____

   _____

4. What does the National Air and Space Museum have to do with time?

   _____

   _____

## Vocabulary Development

1. A **simile** compares two things using the words *like* or *as*. Write the simile used in paragraph 4. _____

   _____

2. An **abbreviation** is a shortened form of a word. Draw lines from the abbreviation to the correct words.

   | District of Columbia | U.S. |
   | United States | NASA |
   | National Air and Space Administration | D.C. |

Write the number of the word that matches its **synonym**.

3. cadet          ____ swept

4. escort         ____ military student

5. beneath       ____ below

6. whisk         ____ guide

## Reading Skills

Write the simple nouns for the possessive nouns below.

1. sister's        _____

2. city's          _____

3. carpenter's     _____

4. subway's        _____

5. Utah's          _____

Check the correct meaning of the underlined word.

6. The subway was <u>riderless</u> today.

   ____ many riders

   ____ less riders

   ____ without riders

7. Francie <u>misused</u> her subway pass.

   ____ used correctly

   ____ used wrong

   ____ used a lot

## Skills Development

Study the sign below and answer the questions.

| Air and Space Museum Locations | |
| --- | --- |
| Einstein Planetarium | 2nd Floor, East |
| Space Lab | 2nd Floor, entry |
| IMAX Theater | 1st Floor, center |
| *Glamorous Glennis* | Ceiling, East |

1. If you wanted to see the plane Chuck Yeager flew, where would you look?

   _____

2. If you were going to see the movie *To Fly!* where would you go?

   _____

3. Where do you need to go to enter the space lab? _____

Tuesday            January 1, 2008

## ISS Ready for Work

### By Sue Spacewalker
*The Zipper Press*

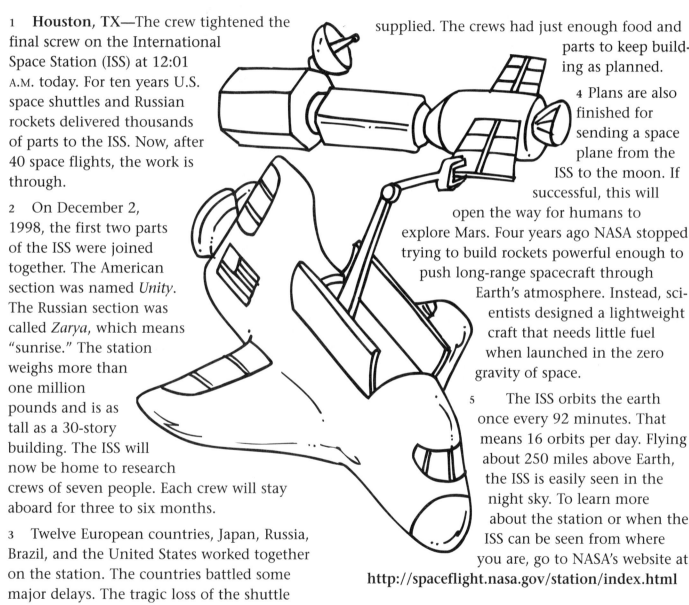

1   **Houston**, TX—The crew tightened the final screw on the International Space Station (ISS) at 12:01 A.M. today. For ten years U.S. space shuttles and Russian rockets delivered thousands of parts to the ISS. Now, after 40 space flights, the work is through.

2   On December 2, 1998, the first two parts of the ISS were joined together. The American section was named *Unity*. The Russian section was called *Zarya*, which means "sunrise." The station weighs more than one million pounds and is as tall as a 30-story building. The ISS will now be home to research crews of seven people. Each crew will stay aboard for three to six months.

3   Twelve European countries, Japan, Russia, Brazil, and the United States worked together on the station. The countries battled some major delays. The tragic loss of the shuttle *Columbia* in 2003 stopped delivery of most parts to the station for over a year. Extraordinary efforts on Earth kept the construction crews supplied. The crews had just enough food and parts to keep building as planned.

4 Plans are also finished for sending a space plane from the ISS to the moon. If successful, this will open the way for humans to explore Mars. Four years ago NASA stopped trying to build rockets powerful enough to push long-range spacecraft through Earth's atmosphere. Instead, scientists designed a lightweight craft that needs little fuel when launched in the zero gravity of space.

5   The ISS orbits the earth once every 92 minutes. That means 16 orbits per day. Flying about 250 miles above Earth, the ISS is easily seen in the night sky. To learn more about the station or when the ISS can be seen from where you are, go to NASA's website at http://spaceflight.nasa.gov/station/index.html

*Sue Spacewalker is a former astronaut and now reports space exploration news for The Zipper Press.*

## Comprehension

1. Number the following events in the order they happened.
   ____ Space shuttle *Columbia* explodes.
   ____ First two sections are joined together.
   ____ Last screw is tightened on ISS.
   ____ Plans are finished for space plane to go to the moon.

2. What force makes launching a ship through the earth's atmosphere so difficult? _____

3. Name a place close to your hometown that takes about $1\frac{1}{2}$ hours to get to by driving in a car. _____

*The ISS would have traveled around the world in the time it took you to go there.*

4. Since the U.S. has more than one shuttle, why do you think NASA waited almost a year before launching another shuttle?
   _____
   _____

## Vocabulary Development

Write the **antonym** for each word below.

1. create _____
2. stay _____
3. major _____
4. sunrise _____
5. together _____

Write the number of the word that best matches its **synonym**.

6. screw          ____ missile
7. design         ____ shuttle
8. examination    ____ read
9. rocket         ____ exploration
10. plane         ____ model
11. read          ____ bolt

## Reading Skills

1. If the prefix **extra-** means "more" or "above and beyond," what does *extraordinary* mean? _____

2. If the prefix **inter-** means "between," what does *international* mean?
   _____

3. If the suffix **-ful** means "full of," what does *successful* mean? _____
   _____

4. What does *powerful* mean? _____
   _____

## Study Skills

Use the chart below to answer the questions.

---

### International Space Station
### Daily Schedule for Dan Morgan
### January 1, 2008

Wake-up Call ...................................................7:00 A.M.
Shower/Dress .............................................7–7:30 A.M.
Breakfast.....................................................7:30–8:00 A.M.
Spacewalk...................................................8:30–11:30 A.M.
Lunch/Rest .................................................12-2:00 P.M.
Exercycle ....................................................2–3:00 P.M.
Experiments................................................4–7:00 P.M.
Dinner/Free time .......................................7–11:00 P.M.
Lights Out ..................................................11:00 P.M.

---

1. What is the reason for this chart?
   _____
   _____

2. What time will astronaut Morgan eat breakfast? _____

3. What part of the day do you think will be the most risky for Dan and why?
   _____
   _____

4. What kind of exercise does Dan get?
   _____

# The Bright Side of the Moon
Keep a picture log of the moon!

> **Full moon, day bright**
> **Black moon, no light.**
> —**Anonymous**

Flip through pages 5–39 of this book while looking at the top right-hand corner. Watch a month of moons fly by!

1   People's first timekeeper was the moon. The wisest men and women in ancient tribes and clans watched its movements in the night sky. On rock walls and deep inside granite caves they carved the moon's progress. Their pictures show how the moon disappears for an entire night. Then it slowly grows to a full moon, only to fade away again.

2   Our ancestors held festivals based on changes in the shape of the moon. They married, danced, and were buried only at certain times. The moon needed to be "right" for each occasion.

## News Alert

An animal bone, carved by a person from the Stone Age, has been found in France. Scientists have dated this bone to **28,000 B.C.** The carvings clearly show the 29-day lunar cycle.

3   The light that radiates from the moon is sunlight reflecting off its surface. The moon *appears* to change shape because as it **orbits**, or rotates, around Earth, different parts are lit by the sun. Only one side of the moon is ever seen from Earth, no matter where you might be watching.

4   The moon is kept in orbit around Earth by the same force that keeps your feet on the ground. This force is **gravity**. It takes 29 days, 12 hours, and 44 minutes for the moon to go around Earth once. This is called a **lunar month**.

## The Phases of the Moon

5   The **new moon** occurs when the moon is positioned between the sun and Earth, with its unlit side facing the Earth. At sunset it may be seen as a very narrow crescent. The next phase is called a **waxing gibbous** moon. This looks like a squashed circle, halfway between a new and a **full moon**. After the full moon occurs, the moonlight starts to wane, or become less. A **waning gibbous** is halfway between full and half. This is followed by a **black moon**, which is invisible from Earth. Finally, the cycle, or phases, begins all over again.

© RBP Books     www.summerbridgeactivities.com     Reading Connection—Grade 4—RBP0199

## Comprehension

1. What keeps the moon from flying off into deep space? _____

2. How do you know the moon was important for our ancestors? Use a sentence from paragraph 1 to help prove your answer.

   _____

   _____

3. Compare a black moon to a full moon. Use the word *while* in your comparison.

   _____

   _____

   _____

4. What do you think "the moon needs to be right" means? _____

   _____

   _____

## Vocabulary Development

Circle the word that does not belong in each row.

1. clans      tribes      loners      families

2. granite    soap        marble      quartz

3. radiates   shines      glows       dims

4. wane       wax         grow        swell

5. wane       wax         fade        decrease

6. ancestors  past        future      parents

Write the number of the word that matches the definition.

7. crescent    ____ not seen

8. invisible   ____ the way in which a thing is placed

9. squashed    ____ a sliver of a circle

10. positioned ____ crushed; battered

## Reading Skills

1. Write the two words that make up the **compound word** *timekeeper*.

   _____

2. Write the meaning of *timekeeper*.

   _____

Write the **possessives** for the following words.

3. cycle    _____

4. men      _____

5. women    _____

6. sky      _____

## Study Skills

The **table of contents** is found near the front of a book. It shows what page each new chapter starts on. Use the table of contents in the chart to answer the questions below.

1. On what page does the story of Galileo begin? _____

2. If you wanted to learn how to make a shadow clock in which chapter should you look? _____

3. How many chapters are there in *Time Measurements*? _____

# Night Animals

Get ready for a nighttime treasure hunt!

1   As you turn off the bedroom light and your parents tuck you in, animals outside your window are starting to wake up. These are creatures of the night, or *nocturnal* animals. Each of these animals has one sense—touch, sight, smell, taste, or hearing—that is unusually suited to night life.

2   Humans are *diurnal*, which means they are mostly awake during the day. To study nocturnal animals you need only a few tools to get started. You'll need a flashlight, a pair of binoculars, a small magnifying glass, a pencil, a pad of paper, and a good afternoon nap!

3   Always remember, **safety first**. Before heading out on your adventure, be sure to get a parent or another adult to go with you. Also, wear closed-toed shoes. You don't want to bump your toes on something you can't see. Not only would it hurt, but you'll scare the animals away while jumping around howling about your sore toe. Ready? Here we go!

## Animals that Crawl

4   Not everyone has a big backyard or a wooded lot close to home. To find creepy crawlers all you need to look for is a small patch of grass, a flower bed, a rotting piece of wood, or a moist rock wedged next to a building. Here you can find snails and slugs, centipedes and millipedes. Best of all, you might find wood lice (also called sow bugs, pill bugs, or roly-polies). These are little black bugs that roll up into a pea-sized ball.

5   The outer coverings of many of these crawlies look crunchy and hard. However, their "skins" are not good at conserving water, and these creatures will quickly dry out and die in the warmth of the day. Use your flashlight to look for a roly-poly under the edge of a patch of lawn.

6   Flash your light around the stems, leaves, and flowers of plants growing in a moist garden. Look for the silvery slime trail that snails and slugs leave behind them as they eat. (They can sometimes devour an entire bed of plants in one night!) This sticky excretion helps protect the bug's soft underside from sharp or rough surfaces.

7   Perhaps you are ready to go back to bed. You'd better hope you have been keeping your room clean. A night creature that lives right inside houses is the bedbug. Found in mattresses and in cracks on walls and floors around a bed, this little insect sucks blood out of a sleeping person. Not too much—just enough to leave a tiny red spot that is very itchy!

8   Maybe your mom or dad have said this short saying to you as they leave your room at night:

> *Night, night*
> *Sleep tight*
> *Don't let the bedbugs bite!*

## Comprehension

1. Why don't humans see very many nocturnal animals? _____
   _____
   _____

2. Roly-polies hide under the edges of lawns during the day. Why do they do this?
   _____
   _____
   _____

3. What might happen to your toes if you wear sandals or go barefoot while exploring at night? _____
   _____
   _____

4. Compare a plant bed and your bed.
   _____
   _____
   _____

## Vocabulary Development

**Homophones** are words that sound exactly the same but have different spellings and meanings. Write the number to match each homophone to its meaning.

1. wood          _____ possessive of *you*

2. would         _____ you are

3. knot          _____ a container

4. not           _____ the past of *be*

5. your          _____ the time from sunset to sunrise

6. you're        _____ a medieval soldier

7. knight        _____ in no way

8. night         _____ the past tense of *will*

9. been          _____ a lump

10. bin          _____ lumber

## Reading Skills

Write the two words that make up the **compound words** found in the paragraph shown in parentheses.

1. (7)  _____
2. (1)  _____
3. (5)  _____
4. (6)  _____
5. (2)  _____
6. (6)  _____
7. (3)  _____
8. (5)  _____

Write the **base word** for the words below.

9. rotting _____

10. mattresses _____

## Study Skills

Study the bar graph Gina made of the different creepy crawlers she found one night in her garden. Answer the questions below.

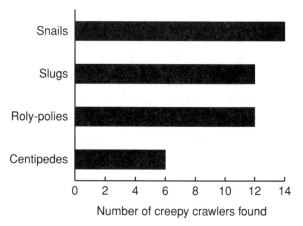

Number of creepy crawlers found

1. Gina found an equal number of which two animals? _____

2. Which animal was found the least? _____
   _____

3. How many snails were found? _____

4. How many slugs and centipedes were found altogether? _____

# The Silent Owl

Can you sleep standing up?

1    Probably the most recognized night bird is the owl. There are over 100 kinds, or species, of owls. The barn, or monkey-faced owl, is found all over the world. It will be the easiest to spot on your late-night animal hunts. Look in old buildings, hollows of trees, holes in rocky cliffs, and, of course, in barns.

> Young owls are called *owlets*.

2    The barn owl grows to be about 15–20 inches tall. It has a white, heart-shaped face and small, black eyes. The barn owl glides soundlessly through the sky on strong, immense wings. Its wings are covered in soft down that smother any noise made by the owl's flight.

3    Rodents make up most of the owl's diet. During cold weather, it also eats small birds. The owl tears its prey into pieces and swallows it in chunks. Later, the owl will regurgitate, or spit out, whatever it can't digest. These balls of bones, feathers, and fur are called *owl pellets*. You can buy them at aviaries across the United States to dissect and examine.

> **Note:** Be sure to wear gloves and a surgical mask when working with owl pellets.

4    In legends, the owl has represented wisdom, power, and the ability to see into the future. During the Middle Ages the owl became associated with witches because of its nighttime hunting habits.

## Hang in There

Have you ever wondered why a sleeping bird doesn't fall off its perch? Maybe not, but this bit of information is quite important to our feathered friends. Muscles in each of the bird's legs tighten and lock its claws in place. What goes on in the bird's brain to make this happen is unknown.

5    When small children are asked to make the sound of an owl, they usually say, "Hoot! Hoot!" While this is a common owl call, there are some interesting exceptions. In the rain forests of Australia the gray sooty owl has a "bomb-whistle" call which sounds like a bomb falling from the sky. The burrowing owl, which lives in abandoned animal holes, imitates a rattlesnake by making a loud buzzing noise. The barn owl has a raspy hiss to warn predators away from its nest.

6    Owls are important to our ecosystem because they keep farms, fields, and homes from being overrun by mice and rats. The following Internet address gives complete instructions on how to build an **owl box** if you want to encourage an owl to roost in your backyard.

www.rain.org/~sals/barnowl.html

© RBP Books    www.summerbridgeactivities.com    Reading Connection—Grade 4—RBP0199

## Comprehension

Write three words or word groups that describe the barn owl.

**1.** _____

**2.** _____

**3.** _____

**4.** What muffles the sound of the owl's beating wings? _____
_____

**5.** What are owl pellets? _____
_____

Write **F** in front of statements that are fact.
Write **O** in front of statements that are opinion.

**6.** ____ The barn owl is the most interesting of all owls.

**7.** ____ Owls regurgitate animal parts they can't digest.

**8.** ____ The sooty owl has a "bomb-whistle" call.

**9.** ____ Owls are a beautiful sight to see.

## Vocabulary Development

Write the number of the word that best fits the definition.

**1.** dissect          ____ differences

**2.** aviaries         ____ perch; resting place

**3.** prey             ____ down

**4.** immense          ____ invaded; occupied

**5.** fluffy feathers  ____ public birdhouses

**6.** associated       ____ to cut apart or divide

**7.** exceptions       ____ abandoned

**8.** deserted         ____ compared to

**9.** overrun          ____ very large; huge

**10.** roost           ____ target; victim

## Reading Skills

Write the **base word** for the words below.

**1.** aviaries    _____

**2.** surgical    _____

**3.** easiest     _____

**4.** burrowing   _____

**5.** carried     _____

**6.** raspy       _____

**7.** tighten     _____

**8.** rocky       _____

**9.** The suffix **-est** means "the most." Write the meaning of *easiest*. _____
_____

**10.** The suffix **-less** means "without." Write the meaning of *soundlessly*. _____
_____

## Study Skills

Write which volume you would use to do research information for each topic.

| Vol 1 | Vol 2 | Vol 3 | Vol 4 | Vol 5 | Vol 6 |
|-------|-------|-------|-------|-------|-------|
| A-D   | E-G   | H-L   | M-P   | R-T   | U-Z   |

**1.** ____ R. Stevenson     **6.** ____ mammals

**2.** ____ woolly bats      **7.** ____ insects

**3.** ____ witches          **8.** ____ zoos

**4.** ____ gardens          **9.** ____ lightning

**5.** ____ echoes           **10.** ____ Bracken Cave

# A Furry Friend

Hurry! What can you use for an umbrella?

1    Bats are flying rodents that are frequently seen in horror movies such as *Dracula* and *Frankenstein*. Scientists who study bats dislike this portrayal. Stories of bats biting humans or getting trapped in someone's long hair are largely untrue. Less than one percent of bats get rabies, a deadly disease more common in dogs. Bats rarely bite people. When they do, it is only in self-defense.

2    In fact, bats are an important part of our ecosystem— just like the owl you read about earlier. There are over 1,000 species of bats. They range from the jelly bean-sized bumblebee bat to the flying fox bat, which has a six-foot wingspan. These mammals are natural ene- mies of night flying insects. Each night the 20 mil- lion Mexican free-tail bats that roost in Bracken Cave in Texas eat up to *200 tons* of insects.

3    Swooping through dark skies, bats use *echolocation* to find their prey. Bats send out high-pitched squeaks and then listen for echoes to bounce back off nearby insects. From what it hears, a bat can sense how big an insect is and in what direction it's moving. Other mam- mals such as dolphins and whales use echolocation to find food deep in the ocean.

4    Farmers are starting to build "bat boxes" in their fields to protect crops from hordes of insects. By encouraging bat colonies to roost on their land, farmers can reduce the amount of chemicals need- ed to kill plant-eating insects. This helps farmers harvest larger, healthier crops.

## Amazing Bat Facts

- African heart-nosed bats can hear an insect walk across a sandy beach from more than six feet away.
- A dozen brown bats can eat 15,000 mosquitoes in an hour.
- The Central American white bat cuts leaves to make "umbrellas" to protect itself from jungle rains.
- Bats have only one baby each year.
- In West Africa the teeny woolly bat lives inside spider webs.
- The body temperature of hibernating North American red bats drops 10 degrees lower than the freezing point of water.
- The pallid bat, which lives in the deserts of North America, eats scorpions and poisonous centipedes, even while getting stung!

    www.summerbridgeactivities.com    **Reading Connection—Grade 4—RBP0199**

## Comprehension

Write **T** in front of the statements that are true.
Write **F** in front of the statements that are false.

1. _____ Bats are dangerous because they frequently bite humans without reason.

2. _____ There is a bat the size of a jelly bean.

3. _____ An enemy of insects is the bat.

4. _____ Humans find their way in the dark by using echolocation.

5. _____ In the winter red bats are as cold as ice cubes.

6. How do bats help farmers?_____

_____

_____

7. Write one fact about bats that you didn't know before reading "A Furry Friend."

_____

_____

_____

8. After reading "A Furry Friend" write your opinion about bats.

   **I think** _____

_____

_____

## Vocabulary Development

Circle the word that does not belong in each row.

1. portrayal      description      photograph

2. dive         swoop       soar      plunge

3. white         rosy        pallid     pale

4. colonies      pairs       groups     flocks

5. mammal       insect      bug       fly

6. clusters      hordes      scatters   groups

## Reading Skills

Write the **compound word** found in the paragraph shown in the parentheses.

1. (2) _____

2. (3) _____

Write the **base word** for each word below.

3. numerous      _____

4. freezing       _____

5. enemies       _____

The prefix **dis-** means "not." Write the meaning of the words below.

6. dislike        _____

7. disease        _____

8. discontent      _____

9. disclaim        _____

## Study Skills

Entry words in a dictionary are divided into **syllables** that show where a word may be divided at the end of a writing line. Breaking a word into syllables also helps with spelling skills. Separate the words below into syllables.

1. numerous      _____

2. dozen         _____

3. temperature    _____

4. ecosystem      _____

5. horror         _____

6. harvest        _____

7. species        _____

8. umbrellas      _____

9. million        _____

10. rodents       _____

# Nature's Flashlights
Could you use a frog for a flashlight?

1   Imagine a beetle so bright that humans used it instead of a candle at night. The cucujo beetle found in Central America is that bug. Native people long ago would tie cucujos to their feet to light their way along steep mountain paths. During summer festivals young girls would decorate their hair with this glowing beetle.

2   The light is produced from a chemical reaction called bioluminescence (*bio-loom-in-es-since*). There are insects, fish, and even some plants that produce this light.

3   Fireflies, or lightning bugs, are found in the eastern United States. (Fireflies are not actually flies. They're beetles.) They are seen on warm evenings in early summer. This beetle is the only insect that can flash its light on and off. The male flashes a pattern of light to females resting on the ground. Think of it as the firefly's way of asking for a date.

> Sometimes frogs eat so many fireflies that they start to glow from the inside out.

4   In the Pacific and Indian Oceans and the Red Sea, flashlight fish live among coral reefs. As the sun sets, they rise to the surface. Smaller fish attracted by the light become easy prey. There is no creature that gives off a brighter light. In fact, fishermen can see the light over 100 feet away!

5   The light is caused by bacteria. The bacteria grow in patches below the fish's eyes and give off a blue-green glow. When trying to avoid a predator, the flashlight fish constantly changes directions as it swims away. To confuse its attacker, it blinks its light on and off. It does this by slipping a cover, like an eyelid, over the shining patches.

6   Other night creatures that glow in the dark are some earthworms, anchovies, jellyfish, squid, and the railroad worm. A fungus or mushroom called the yellow jack-o-lantern produces a bright greenish light. But don't eat it ... it's poisonous.

   www.summerbridgeactivities.com    **Reading Connection—Grade 4—RBP0199**

## Comprehension

1. If a frog glows in the dark, what is your prediction of what might happen to that frog? _____
   _____
   _____

2. What really glows, the bacteria or the flashlight fish? _____

3. The flashlight fish looks like it is blinking on and off. What is the cause? _____
   _____
   _____

4. Why is the firefly not a fly? _____
   _____

## Vocabulary Development

1. Write the word that means "a light made by insects, fish, and plants." Then say it aloud three times.
   _____

Check the correct meaning of the underlined word.

2. This is a firefly's way of asking for a <u>date</u>.
   ____ a piece of fruit
   ____ going out with a friend

3. Fishermen <u>fish</u> for fish.
   ____ the act of hunting for fish
   ____ an animal that lives in water

Match the number of the word to its **synonym**.

4. celebrations   ____ germ
5. practice       ____ avoid
6. bacteria       ____ produced
7. predator       ____ festivals
8. made           ____ deadly
9. poisonous      ____ custom
10. escape        ____ attacker

## Reading Skills

Write the **base word** for each word below.

1. attacker    _____
2. brightest   _____
3. patches     _____
4. eaten       _____
5. shining     _____

Write the four **compound words** in paragraph 6.

6. _____
7. _____
8. _____
9. _____

## Study Skills

Circle the word in each column that fits between the guide words.

1. **obtain-odd**
   observe
   oboe
   ocean

2. **bedbug-began**
   because
   beetle
   begin

3. **fumble-fur**
   fungus
   fuss
   full

4. **cheese-cherry**
   cheery
   chest
   chemical

5. Number the words below in alphabetical order.
   ____ firefly      ____ summer
   ____ flashes      ____ eyelid
   ____ seen         ____ eat
   ____ states       ____ festival

# The Scent of Night
Yummy...the sweet smell of rotting meat.

1 A scent ... an aroma ... a smell. This is all a moth needs to find one of the many flowers that bloom as the sun sets. Unlike colorful butterflies or honeybees, the drab hawk moth and the little brown bat seek nectar at night.

2 Plants that flower by day need *diurnal* animals to help with pollination. Plants that bloom at night plants rely on *nocturnal* animals for the same reason. Pollen is a powdery substance inside flowers. *Pollination* occurs when pollen is moved from a flower on one plant to a flower on another plant. Without pollination, plants can not make seeds for the next year. Most brightly colored flowers close their petals at night to keep their pollen dry. In the morning, after the night's dew has evaporated, the petals reopen. They are ready again for visits from tiny insects and birds.

Take a visit to a garden at sunset. If you are lucky, you might see a daytime bug that has been trapped in a flower as its petals closed. Don't worry. The bug will be snug until the next morning.

3 Night-blooming flowers come in shades of pale white, yellow, and pink. They lack the dazzling colors of day bloomers because animals are not attracted to them by sight. Animals find these flowers by smell. Their fragrance during the day is often faint or unnoticeable. At night, however, a single blossom can fill an entire garden with its scent.

## Honeysuckle

4 This vine has trumpet-shaped flowers and grows wild all over the world. Its creamy white and yellow blossoms make a gourmet meal for the hawk moth. Like the butterfly, this moth has a long proboscis that is perfect for sipping the flower's honey-flavored nectar.

5 If you have a honeysuckle plant near your house, visit it on a warm, moonlit night. Carefully remove a blossom by pinching off the slender stem at the bottom of the flower. With your fingernail, nip the green base of the flower in half. Gently pull back on the base until you see a drop of liquid. This is the flower's nectar.

## Wild Banana Flower

6 Most night-flowering plants are pleasant for humans to smell. But there are some you just don't want to get near. The purple-brownish flower of the wild banana has rust colored pollen. By its second day of blooming it has a scent that reminds people of rotting meat. Silky brown bats are so attracted by this smell that they sometimes get trapped inside the flower's huge, stinky petals when they close at sunrise. What a way to spend the day!

www.summerbridgeactivities.com   Reading Connection—Grade 4—RBP0199

## Comprehension

1. The wild banana flower stinks. What is the effect?_____
_____

2. Do *nocturnal* or *diurnal* animals pollinate night-blooming plants?_____
_____

3. Why are night-blooming plants so pale?
_____
_____

4. What helps the hawk moth get nectar out of the honeysuckle flower? _____
_____

5. Why do you think day-blooming plants need to keep their pollen dry? (Hint: Think of how the powdery pollen is transported.)
_____
_____

6. The author has two opinions in paragraph 6. Write one of them. _____
_____

## Vocabulary Development

Write the number of the word in front of its definition.

1. drab        ____ special, tasty

2. dew         ____ to look for something

3. stinky      ____ a reddish-brown color

4. evaporate   ____ condensation; drops of water

5. fragrance   ____ to clip or snip

6. seek        ____ to dry up

7. rely        ____ to be smelly

8. gourmet     ____ scent; aroma

9. nip         ____ colorless

10. rust       ____ to depend on

## Reading Skills

1. If the suffix **re-** means "do again," what does *reopen* mean? _____
_____

2. If the suffix **un-** means "not," what does the word *unnoticeable* mean? _____
_____

Write the three **compound words** found in paragraph 5.

3. _____

4. _____

5. _____

Write the two **compound words** in paragraph 1.

6. _____

7. _____

## Study Skills

Complete the following outline. Use paragraph 2 for Part I. Use paragraph 3 for Part II and paragraph 5 for Part III.

I.  Plant pollination
    A. Diurnal animals help pollinate day-blooming plants.
    B. _____
    C. Both types of animals move pollen from one plant to another.

II.  Night-blooming plants
    A. _____
    B. _____
    C. _____

III.  Finding honeysuckle nectar
    A. First, remove blossom
    B. Next, _____
    C. Then, _____

# A Night Poet

Have you ever felt the breath of Bogies in your hair?

## The Land of Nod

From breakfast on all through the day
At home among my friends I stay;
But every night I go abroad
Afar into the land of Nod.

All by myself I have to go,
With none to tell me what to do—
All alone beside the streams
And up the mountains-sides of dreams.

The strangest things are there for me,
Both things to eat and things to see,
And many frightening sights abroad
Till morning in the Land of Nod.

Try as I like to find the way,
I never can get back by day,
Nor can remember plain and clear
The curious music that I hear.

Robert Louis Stevenson (1850–1894) wrote the timeless adventure books *Kidnapped* and *Treasure Island*. Published in the 1885, Stevenson's collection of poems, *A Child's Garden of Verses*, contains some of the best known nighttime poetry ever written. Below are three poems.

## Shadow March (from "North-West Passage")

All round the house is the jet-black night;
It stares through the window-pane;
It crawls in the corners, hiding from the light,
And it moves with the moving flame.

Now my little heart goes a-beating like a drum,
With the breath of the Bogies in my hair;
And all round the candle the crooked
        shadows come,
And go marching along up the stair.
The shadows of the balusters, the shadow of
        the lamp,
The shadow of the child that goes to bed—
All the wicked shadows coming, tramp, tramp,
        tramp,
With the black night overhead.

## The Moon

The moon has a face like the clock in the hall.
She shines on the thieves on the garden wall,
On streets and fields and harbor quays,
And birdies asleep in the forks of trees.

The squalling cat and the squeaking mouse,
The howling dog by the door of the house,
the bat that lies in bed at noon,
All love to be out by the light of the moon.

But all of the things that belong to the day
Cuddle to sleep to be out of her way;
And flowers and children close their eyes
Till up in the morning the sun shall rise.

## Comprehension

When you are asked to write a **comparison**, you are being asked to tell how two things are alike or not alike. The word *while* is frequently used when making comparisons.

1. Compare the dog and the mouse in the poem "The Moon." _____

_____

_____

2. Compare the sights and the music in "The Land of Nod." _____

_____

_____

3. Circle what the child is doing when she is in "The Land of Nod."

  playing          eating          dreaming

4. **a.** In "Shadow March" what is the child afraid of?_____

  **b.** Name two things the jet-black night does in "Shadow March." _____

_____

_____

5. How old was Robert Louis Stevenson when *A Child's Garden of Verses* was published?

_____

## Vocabulary Development

Write the number of the word that best matches its **synonym**.

1. balusters        ____ odd

2. squall           ____ set

3. bogie            ____ pillars

4. collection       ____ away

5. curious          ____ yell

6. abroad           ____ monster

## Reading Skills

Write the **possessive** for the following words.

1. flame        _____

2. it           _____

3. birdie       _____

4. music        _____

5. thief        _____

6. Find the **compound word** in the introduction to the poems. _____

## Study Skills

Read the directions below; then answer the questions.

> # Notice
>
> Before going to bed at night, the nanny must make sure that she reads the child one story and one poem. (Nothing of a scary nature will be allowed.) Teeth and hands of the child must be checked for cleanliness before tucking into bed. Finally, all night candles in the children's bedrooms are to be blown out and then spit on.

1. Who are these directions for?

_____

2. Would "Shadow March" be a good poem for the nanny to read aloud to the children? Why or why not?_____

_____

_____

3. Name two things the nanny is to do with the candles.

_____

_____

# Answer Pages

## Page 6

### Comprehension
1. F
2. T
3. T
4. T
5. F
6. Time is definite moment, fixed by a clock or calendar.
7. Sentences will vary.

### Vocabulary Development
1. past
2. forward
3. right
4. down
5. a. smart
6. b. measurement
7. c. above normal

### Reading Skills
1. ran, run
2. ate, eat
3. jumped, jump
4. slept, sleep
5. read, read
6. spoke, speak
7. danced, dance
8. walked, walk
9. jogged, jog

### Study Skills
1. C. The third—a cube, D. The fourth—time
2. B. Theory of Relativity
   C. future time travel

## Page 8

### Comprehension
1. in the brain
2. It would be winter. It's cold, snowy and dark.
3. an imaginary pole
4. Winter is coming.
5. The earth is rotating away from the sun.
6. There are 24 hours in a day.
7. Greenland, Canada

### Vocabulary Development
1. eastern, western
2. 8
3. 10
4. 7
5. 3
6. 9
7. 5
8. 6
9. 2
10. 4

### Reading Skills
1. without end
2. after - noon
3. after 12:00 P.M.
4. countries
5. geese
6. mice
7. children
8. moose

### Study Skills
1. No. Boys & girls over age 12 play on separate teams.
2. There are only 30 days in April.
3. May 31, 2004

## Page 10

### Comprehension
1. India
2. Scottish
3. Answers will vary.
4. rocky
5. He received an excellent eduction. The lighthouses were magnificent.

### Vocabulary Development
1. pencil
2. Germany
3. pen
4. sunset
5. playmate
6. calm
7. nights
8. horrible, terrible
9. worst
10. poor

### Reading Skills
1. bad fortune
2. badly informed
3. behave badly
4. lead badly
5. handle badly
6. *Scot* and *land*
7. *coast* and *line*
8. *light* and *house*

### Study Skills
I-III. Answers will vary.

## Page 12

### Comprehension
1. No one studied the sky until Galileo in the sixteenth century.
2. Jeudi
3. Sun, Mercury, Venus, Moon, Mars, Jupiter, Saturn
4. the Koran
5. Monday
6. loving & giving
7. Monday is named after the moon, which has a white face.

### Vocabulary Development
1. C
2. F
3. A
4. E
5. D
6. B

### Reading Skills
1. Sunday
2. throughout
3. without
4. more small
5. more great

### Study Skills
1. B. About 1600 B.C. days are created.
2. B. Ancients thought the sun was a planet.

# Answer Pages

## Page 14

### Comprehension
1. b. <u>Runes are ancient symbols used to write messages and protect people.</u>
2. Scots bowed to the new moon and jingled money in their pockets.
3. Answers will vary. To find courage is to be brave even when you don't want to be.

### Vocabulary Development
1. Babylonians
2. superstition
3. mythical
4. turban
5. worship
6. legend
7. jingle

### Reading Skills
1. wise and old
2. ancient
3. huge
4. gigantic
5. early
6. ancient
7. enormous and blue
8. country
9. courage

### Study Skills
1. Tuesday
2. Celsius
3. Scotland

## Page 16

### Comprehension
1. *Mercari* means to trade and the first four letters are *merc*.
2. Answers will vary.
3. Venus is a planet, not a distant sun.
4. Answers will vary. Odin was the most powerful god, while Thor was the strongest.

### Vocabulary Development
1. 4
2. 5
3. 7
4. 6
5. 3
6. 2
7. 1
8. 9
9. 8

### Reading Skills
1. named
2. place
3. struck
4. touched
5. rises
6. harvested
7. lived
8. came
9. passed, throwing
10. carried

### Study Skills
1. morn•ing
2. un•known
3. pur•ple
4. mar•i•gold
4. mer•chants
6. plan•et
7. Ju•pi•ter
8. thun•der•bolt
9. Thurs•day
10. an•cient

## Page 18

### Comprehension
1. F
2. T
3. T
4. T
5. F
6. Answers will vary. Saturn can bring death while also bringing strength.
7. The weekend days are Saturday and Sunday.
8. north

### Vocabulary Development
1. medicine
2. young
3. plain
4. modern
5. rough
6. bore
7. planet
8. silly

### Reading Skills
1. a sharp curved blade
2. a poisonous purple flower
3. acts both good and bad

### Study Skills
1. <u>The Sun did the Earth a favor by warming her cold mountains.</u>
2. Answers will vary.
3. noun

## Page 20

### Comprehension
1. Sosigenes
2. the time it takes for the moon to rotate around Earth
3. 100
4. He removed ten days from the calendar in 1583.
5. An astronomer studies stars and planets.

### Vocabulary Development
1. smooth
2. ~~sun~~ solution
3. summer
4. fall
5. happy/sane
6. plant
7. small
8. accurate
9. angry
10. Answers will vary.

### Reading Skills
1. 365 days and 6 hours.
2. calendar introduced by Julius Caesar
3. calendar introduced by Pope Gregory
4. a big mess

### Study Skills
1. 45 A.D.
2. 2000
3–4. Answers will vary.

# Answer Pages

## Page 22

### Comprehension
1, 2, 4, 3

### Vocabulary Development
1. interview
2. discuss
3. explained
4. bothered
5. identical
6. fourth
7. calendar
8. holiday
9. unjust
10. designed

### Reading Skills
1. *worlds* and *day*
2. *through* and *out*
3. *time* and *table*
4. *birth* and *day*

### Study Skills
1. Monday, April 11, 1955
2. Samantha Warts
3. *The Daily Post*
4. The Zipper Press

## Page 24

### Comprehension
1. 3, 1, 2, 4
2. 40 years old
3. Bill doesn't grow much older, <u>while</u> Bill gets twenty years older. Answers will vary.

### Vocabulary Development
1. past
2. sea
3. thyme
4. cry
5. carrot
6. awesome
7. idea

### Reading Skills
1. relative
2. different
3. study
4. fast
5. spaceship's
6. apple's
7. children's
8. Einstein's

### Study Skills
1. B. the Theory of Relativity.
2. A. speed of light.
   B. 186,000 miles per second.
3. A. how fast you go.
   B. slower time passes.

## Page 26

### Comprehension
1–6. Answers will vary.

### Vocabulary Development
1. a kind of fruit
2. to not eat food for a period of time
3. to grow old

### Reading Skills
1. *street* and *car*
2. *bare* and *foot*
3. without friends
4. without a home
5. without hope
6. without help

### Study Skills
1. my last name
2. three
3. my signature

## Page 28

### Comprehension
1. O
2. O
3. F
4. Answers will vary.
   The shadow clock needs sunlight, while the water clock can work in darkness.

### Vocabulary Development
1. bored
2. end
3. moonlight/dark
4. modern
5. sunrise
6. inventive
7. mechanical
8. millennium
9. Egyptian

### Reading Skills
1. afternoon
2. pinhole
3. nighttime
4. Egyptian's
5. clocks'

### Study Skills
1. 1492
2. New York City
3. No Bother Airlines
4. 10:17 A.M.

© RBP Books    www.summerbridgeactivities.com    Reading Connection—Grade 4—RBP0199

# Answer Pages

## Page 30

**Comprehension**
1. People used powdered eggshells instead of sand.
2. Answers will vary: nails, tacks, pebbles
3. The rocking motion caused by big waves made the pendulums crash.

**Vocabulary Development**
1. keep time
2. over time
3. embedded
4. intervals
5. incense
6. bulb
7. pendulum
8. aboard
9. scents

**Reading Skills**
1. breeze, air current
2. bubble, cook
3. darkness
4. new feathers

**Study Skills**
1. 801
2. old hourglasses
3. $1,000
4. We don't know.

## Page 32

**Comprehension**
1. 4, 1, 5, 3, 2
2. The children fall asleep.
3. The mouth of the jar is too small.
4. the heat from the sunlight

**Vocabulary Development**
1. 8
2. 4
3. 6
4. 1
5. 7
6. 2
7. 5
8. 3

**Reading Skills**
1. cycle
2. century
3. sprinkle
4. mark
5. everyone's
6. substance's
7. jar's
8. carton's

**Study Skills**
1. 2, 1, 3
2. 3, 2, 1
3. 2, 1, 3
4. 2, 1, 3
5. re•cy•cla•ble
6. the•saur•us
7. dic•tion•ary
8. chal•lenge
9. di•rec•tions
10. plas•tic

## Page 34

**Comprehension**
1. to tell about biological clocks
2. Your biological clock is different.
3. inside your body
4. Cycles of nature, such as day and night.

**Vocabulary Development**
1. when the sun is farthest south, or the shortest daylight of the year
2. 5
3. 6
4. 3
5. 4
6. 2

**Reading Skills**
1. "hasn't caught up to…"
2. Paris's
3. jet's
4. doctors'
5. zone's
6. study's

**Study Skills**
1. 10:00 P.M.
2. 3
3. yes
4. 6:00 A.M.

## Page 36

**Comprehension**
1. a bell
2. a rod
3. Answers will vary. Women wore long dresses and boots with heels. They could easily trip.
4. Both were big.
5. Answers may vary: gears turning.

**Vocabulary Development**
1. bump
2. digs
3. daughter
4. basement
5. unknown
6. noisy
7. commoner
8. a round step
9. a lengthy period

**Reading Skills**
1. wound again
2. in an extreme way
3. in a simple way
4. in the usual way
5. it•self

**Study Skills**
1. ton
2. 1½ tons, 1.5 tons
3. 62 − 49 = 13 years between
4. 350 − 200 = 150 steps

# Answer Pages

## Page 38

### Comprehension
1. Answers will vary.
2. The birds were heavy and bothersome. Answers will vary.
3. Einstein's Theory of Relativity—time travel

### Vocabulary Development
1. embellished
2. repose
3. relieved
4. unknown
5. ecstatic
6. recognize
7. William Shakespeare
8. their
9. they're

### Reading Skills
1. *no* and *body*
2. *home* and *town*
3. oxen
4. children
5. women
6. men

### Study Skills
1. Writing Limericks
2. 46–50
3. 1–12
4. Edward Lear's Short Stories, Chapter Four

## Page 40

### Comprehension
1. F
2. T
3. T
4. F
5. They were test planes, and the Air Force didn't want people to steal ideas. Answers will vary.
6. Johnny's mom was sad the boys were dying.

### Vocabulary Development
1. windows lying on the ground like fallen snow
2. "came over the air"
3. calm
4. elite
5. greasy
6. fiery
7. descended
8. barrier

### Reading Skills
1. *week* and *day*
2. *week* and *ends*
3. *air* and *craft*
4. *school* and *house*
5. *class* and *room*
6. *base* and *ball*
7. fall
8. dust
9. whiz
10. tap

### Study Skills
1. Oct. 14
2. Oct. 16
3. doesn't say
4. 90° F

## Page 42

### Comprehension
1. start from scratch
2. month of Sundays
3. dog days of August
4. jump the gun
5. dilly-dally

### Vocabulary Development
1. pledge
2. enemy
3. time
4. overlook
5. planet
6. follower
7. play
8. pig

### Reading Skills
1. behave
2. friend
3. school
4. fame
5. laugh
6. happy
7. label
8. glory

### Study Skills
1. braid
2. gondola
3. lists
4. spray
5. moon
6. flash
7. world
8. certain

## Page 44

### Comprehension
1. F
2. O
3. F
4. O
5. O
6. F

### Vocabulary Development
1. expensive
2. nowadays
3. immigrants
4. blacksmith
5. evening
6. photo

### Reading Skills
1. blacksmith's
2. student's
3. horse's
4. immigrant's
5. blacksmith
6. sometimes
7. handmade
8. sunset
9. fireplace
10. nighttime

### Study Skills
1. swat-swizzle
2. deduce-demand
3. wing-winter
4. canal-cannon
5. iris-Iroquois

© RBP Books    www.summerbridgeactivities.com    Reading Connection—Grade 4—RBP0199

# Answer Pages

## Page 46

### Comprehension
1. the blacksmith
2. He needs to think of her once more, now in grave she lies.
3. A blacksmith's life is like the ticking of a clock.
4. cried   5. sing   6. evening

### Vocabulary Development
1. sexton
2. threshing
3. chaff
4. repose
5. parson
6. sinewy

### Reading Skills
1. pre- to wash before
2. pre- before school
3. pre- before a game
4. pre- to view before
5. pre- before a war
6. pre- before a date
7. preschool
8. pregame

### Study Skills
1. general store
2. north
3. west toward the church
4. southeast

## Page 48

### Comprehension
1. Galileo is one of the most brilliant men to have ever lived.
2. No, because Galileo was kicked out of the university for proving Aristotle wrong.
3. You can feel your heartbeat by finding your pulse in your wrist. He used his steady heartbeat to time the lantern's swings.
4. to tell about part of Galileo's life.

### Vocabulary Development
1. E
2. D
3. C
4. B
5. A
6. Galileo
7. Pisa

### Reading Skills
1. not correct
2. not popular
3. not happy
4. not wanted
5. not loaded
6. fingernail
7. heartbeat
8. meatballs

### Study Skills
1. Answers will vary.
2. Right
3. Right

## Page 50

### Comprehension
1. celandine
2. elk
3. migration
4. daylight
5. Answers will vary. Both Shoshones and shepherds migrate.
6. A miracle of nature is something about nature we don't understand.

### Vocabulary Development
1. cattle—steer
2. none
3. garden—field
4. store—shop
5. 6
6. 8
7. 5
8. 10
9. 7
10. 9

### Reading Skills
1. visitor
2. migrate
3. north
4. south
5. roofless, without a roof
6. rebuild, to build again

### Study Skills
1. south
2. Oregon
3. north or northwest
4. Answers will vary.

## Page 52

### Comprehension
1. Don't be greedy.
2. Pay attention to what you are doing.
3. She shakes her head.
4. There are too many nuts in her hand.
5. I'll smile sweetly and shake my head from side to side.

### Vocabulary Development
1. died   2. pail   3. mind

### Reading Skills
1. cream
2. grab
3. real
4. stubborn
5. bulge
6. honey
7. dust
8. spy
9. sweet
10. broke

### Study Skills
1. adjective
2. Sentences will vary.
3. three
4. one
5. to hold in balance
6. verb

# Answer Pages

## Page 54

### Comprehension
1. Hot. He could not resist the cool water.
2. The raven was close to dying and was running out of time to find water <u>by sunset</u>.
3. desperate
4. disc

### Vocabulary Development
1. temptation
2. fleshy
3. cottonwood
4. current
5. withered

### Reading Skills
1. octopi
2. bronchi
3. fungi
4. nimbi
5. radii
6. sweetest, most sweet
7. softest, most soft
8. darkest, most dark
9. fullest, most full
10. lightest, most light

### Study Skills
1. fables
2. morals
3. 3, 8, 9, 6, 1          4, 7, 10, 2, 5

## Page 56

### Comprehension
1. wings, fly, 80 miles, Cerro Pelon, winter, rest, March, North, eggs, die
2. Answers will vary. Because it contains a sticky white fluid.
3. Its population would decrease or become extinct because the caterpillar will only eat milkweed.

### Vocabulary Development
1. bothersome
2. soaring
3. substance
4. nectar
5. equipped
6. transparent
7. huddled

### Reading Skills
1. butter, flies
2. day, light
3. pin, head
4. milk, weed
5. a straw-like mouth

### Study Skills
1. Answers will vary.
2. page 20
3. The Mystery Continues

## Page 58

### Comprehension
1. Mrs. Whatsit once was a star.
2. The fifth dimension is when there is no time between the present and future.
3. A group of people are fighting the Black Thing.
4. Answers will vary.

### Vocabulary Development
1. rein
2. won
3. hour
4. people

### Reading Skills
1. planets'
2. travelers'
3. hostages'
4. books'
5. brothers'
6. the state of being dark
7. the state of being fond
8. the state of being easy

### Study Skills
1. 1
2. 3
3. 5
4. 6

## Page 60

### Comprehension
1. The thunder woke her, and then she wanted to go outside; or, she wanted to count the fawn's spots.
2. Answers will vary.
3. Answers will vary.
4. Answers will vary.

### Vocabulary Development
1. terrible
2. desire
3. experts
4. saved

### Reading Skills
1. brothers'
2. Rose's
3. lodge's
4. sisters'
5. engineers'
6. children's
7. deer's
8. baby's
9. winter, berry or white-spotted Answers will vary: a bush covered in berries during the winter.

### Study Skills
1. fawn
2. moss
3. scent
4. delicate

# Answer Pages

## Page 62

### Comprehension
1. four
2. Answers will vary.
3. The spots were tomato sauce.
4. The cards were dusty because Rose wasn't using them.
5. Answers will vary.

### Vocabulary Development
1. quiet
2. singing
3. parting
4. orderly
5. leave
6. apples
7. going

### Reading Skills
1. eating with a bunch of earthlings
2. in case a water hose breaks
3. spun a webful of eggs
4. Answers will vary.
5. Answers will vary.
6. any state outside the state you live in

### Study Skills
1. Moss Landing
2. 5:00 P.M.
3. knock softly
4. nothing, no school

## Page 64

### Comprehension
1. The early birds get the worm.
2. She calls them night owls because they stay up late.
3. The squirrel was hungry and used most of its fat during hibernation.
4. (Answers will vary) Rose woke with the sunrise and fell asleep with the sunset. (Clocks just didn't work for her anymore than they would for bears.)
5. (Answers will vary)Rose felt pride when she realized she was very good at something, understanding nature.

### Vocabulary Development
1. ambled
2. glen
3. primrose
4. hibernation

### Reading Skills
1. hibernate
2. berry
3. appear
4. not appearing
5. not approve
6. not like
7. not loyal
8. not tasteful

### Study Skills
1. northeast
2. southeast
3. Merced River
4. east

## Page 66

### Comprehension
1. 3, 1, 2, 4
2. It means "what have you been doing?"
3. Answers will vary.
4. Answers will vary.

### Vocabulary Development
1. right
2. ruler
3. match
4. collage

### Reading Skills
1. early
2. late
3. long
4. activity
5. birthday
6. timeline

### Study Skills
1. boil 4 cups water
2. 1/4 teaspoon salt
3. 3 tablespoons

## Page 68

### Comprehension
1. No. The prize was an all-expense-paid trip.
2. They were tired after seeing the Air and Space Museum.
3. Answers will vary.
4. Answers will vary. Time is movement through space.

### Vocabulary Development
1. The city's monuments were like shimmering jewels.
2. District of Columbia—D.C.
United States—U.S.
National Air and Space Administration—NASA

6, 3, 5, 4

### Reading Skills
1. sister
2. city
3. carpenter
4. subway
5. Utah
6. without riders
7. used wrong

### Study Skills
1. Ceiling, East
2. 1st Floor, Center
3. 2nd Floor

# Answer Pages

## Page 70

### Comprehension
1. 2, 1, 4, 3    2. gravity
3. Answers will vary.
4. Answers will vary; e.g.: fear, safety, no astronauts want to fly, etc.

### Vocabulary Development
1. destroy    2. go
3. minor    4. sunset
5. apart
   9, 10, 11, 8, 7, 6

### Reading Skills
1. beyond the ordinary
2. between nations
3. full of success
4. full of power

### Study Skills
1. For Dan Morgan to see what time he is to do certain things.
2. 7:30–8:00 A.M.
3. Answers will vary.
4. He uses an exercycle.

## Page 72

### Comprehension
1. gravity
2. The wisest men and women were given the task to watch the moon. *or* On rock walls and deep inside granite caves they covered the moon's progress.
3. A black moon is invisible, while a full moon is completely visible.
4. The moon needed to be a certain shape before events could happen.

### Vocabulary Development
1. loners    2. soap
3. dims    4. wane
5. wax    6. future
7. 8    8. 10
9. 7    10. 9

### Reading Skills
1. time keeper    2. a keeper of time
3. cycle's    4. men's
5. women's    6. sky's

### Study Skills
1. 22
2. 2
3. 5

## Page 74

### Comprehension
1. Because humans are diurnal, or awake in the day, while nocturnal animals are up a night.
2. The "skins" of roly-polies aren't good at conserving water, so they need to hide from the sun.
3. Answers will vary.
4. Answers will vary.

### Vocabulary Development
1. 5    2. 6    3. 10    4. 9
5. 8    6. 7    7. 4    8. 2
9. 3    10. 1

### Reading Skills
1. bed, bug    2. bed, room
3. how, ever    4. some, times
5. flash, light    6. under, side
7. some, thing    8. flash, light
9. rot    10. mattress

### Study Skills
1. slugs and roly-polies    2. the centipede
3. 14    4. 18

## Page 76

### Comprehension
1–3. Answers will vary.
     white heart-shaped face; 15-20 inches tall; immense wings; small, black eyes
4. The soft down on its wings.
5. Balls of fur, feathers and bones that the owl spits out.
6. O    7. F    8. F    9. O

### Vocabulary Development
1. 7    2. 10    3. 5    4. 9
5. 2    6. 1    7. 8    8. 6
9. 4    10. 3

### Reading Skills
1. aviary    2. surgery
3. easy    4. burrow
5. carry    6. rasp
7. tight    8. rock
9. the most easy    10. without a sound

### Study Skills
1. 5    2. 1    3. 6    4. 2
5. 2    6. 4    7. 3    8. 6
9. 3    10. 1

www.summerbridgeactivities.com    Reading Connection—Grade 4—RBP0199

# Answer Pages

## Page 78

### Comprehension
1. F          2. T          3. T
4. F          5. T
6. Bats help farmers by eating plant-eating insects.
7. Answers will vary.
8. Answers will vary.

### Vocabulary Development
1. photograph          2. soar
3. rosy                4. pairs
5. mammal              6. scatters

### Reading Skills
1. bumblebee           2. echolocation or nearby
3. number              4. freeze
5. enemy               6. not like
7. not at ease         8. not content
9. not claim

### Study Skills
1. nu•mer•ous          2. doz•en
3. tem•per•a•ture      4. e•co•sys•tem
5. hor•ror             6. har•vest
7. spe•cies            8. um•brel•las
9. mil•lion            10. ro•dents

## Page 80

### Comprehension
1. Answers will vary: easier for a predator to see and attack
2. the bacteria
3. A cover, like an eyelid, slides up and down over the bacteria patch.
4. A firefly is a beetle.

### Vocabulary Development
1. bioluminescence
2. going out with a friend
3. the act of hunting for fish
4. 6     5. 10    6. 8     7. 4
8. 9     9. 5     10. 7

### Reading Skills
1. attack      2. bright      3. patch
4. eat         5. shine       6. jellyfish
7. railroad    8. earthworm   9. mushroom

### Study Skills
1. ocean          2. fungus
3. beetle         4. chemical
5. 4, 5, 6, 7     8, 2, 1, 3

## Page 82

### Comprehension
1. The silky brown bat is attracted to it.
2. nocturnal animals
3. They don't need any color because they attract by smell, not sight.
4. its proboscis
5. If the pollen was wet it would be in a clump and wouldn't stick.
6. 1. What a way to spend the day!
   2. There are some you just don't want to get near.

### Vocabulary Development
1. 8     2. 6     3. 10    4. 2
5. 9     6. 4     7. 3     8. 5
9. 1     10. 7

### Reading Skills
1. open again          2. not noticeable
3. honeysuckle         4. moonlit
5. fingernail   6. butterflies   7. honeybees

### Study Skills
I. B. Nocturnal animals pollinate night-blooming plants.
II. A. pale in color
    B. attract animals by scent
    C. fragrant at night
III. B. Next, nip green base in half.
     C. Then, pull back until nectar appears.

## Page 84

### Comprehension
1. The dog howls while the mouse squeaks.
2. The sights are frightening while the music is curious.
3. dreaming          4. a. shadows, night
5. 35 years old         b. stares, crawls, moves

### Vocabulary Development
1. 5     2. 4     3. 1
4. 6     5. 2     6. 3

### Reading Skills
1. flame's     2. its       3. birdie's
4. music's     5. thief's   6. nighttime

### Study Skills
1. the nanny
2. No, it wouldn't because the nanny is not to read anything scary.
3. blow them out and spit on them

# Notes

Five things I'm thankful for:

1. _____
2. _____
3. _____
4. _____
5. _____

# Notes

Five things I'm thankful for:

1. _____
2. _____
3. _____
4. _____
5. _____